Byker
and Lower Ouseburn

Alan Morgan

ISBN: 9781857951639

Illustrations from the collection of Newcastle Libraries, unless otherwise stated.
Modern photographs taken by Alan Morgan, 2016.

Published by:
City of Newcastle Upon Tyne
Newcastle Libraries
Tyne Bridge Publishing, 2016
www.tynebridgepublishing.co.uk
Design: David Hepworth
Image research: Shawn Fairless

Front Cover: A photograph of Avondale Road is as it appeared in the late 60s. At the top of the bank is St Peter's Road with some of Raby Street's original buildings visible at the bottom, including part of the school. A few of the houses on the left of the photograph at the corner of St Peter's Road survive but everything else, apart from the superb view towards Newcastle and the river, has changed including the road layout. The neighbourhood is now known as St Michael's Mount.

Title page: A 1976 view looking up part of Raby Street, the principal street of old Byker, with shops, houses and public transport, towards what would have been Shields Road but now blocked by the recently completed Byker Wall. This part of the multi-storied wall is known as Raby Gate and is one of several access points throughout its length of nearly one mile. All other buildings have been replaced by mainly low-rise dwellings on either side of a much narrower 'access only' thoroughfare. Further down the street at Raby Cross a few retail businesses are clustered together. The Hare and Hounds pub, run by Newcastle Breweries since 1892, has also been demolished and its corner site with Mason Street now grassed over.

Contents

Upper Byker in the late 60s including St Michael's Church from Raby Street school alongside St Michael's Road.

4

Introduction

For the purpose of this book, the suburb of Byker in the east end of Newcastle is defined as being bordered to the north by Shields Road and the Fossway, to the east by Walker, to the south by the Tyne and to the west by the Ouseburn Valley. The suburb has then been divided into four geographical chapters to assist in the visiting of sites.

Byker is one of the very few Northumbrian place names with Scandinavian roots (most are of Anglo-Saxon origin) and translates as 'the settlement by the marsh'. The name probably dates from the 800s at a time when there were frequent Viking raids up the Tyne, although it first appears in records in 1196 when it is called Bilkere.

In 1198 William of Byker was named as holder of the serjeanty (assistant) to the Sheriff of Northumberland for the area between the rivers Tyne and Coquet, judged to be the most important in the county. It is thought he obtained this position as a result of his marriage to Margery of Byker, the widow and heiress of the previous holder of the office. William's earlier name had been William Escolland.

William's duty in his new post included the issue of writs and the collection of debts on behalf of the king, the guarding of beasts and chattels taken in settlement of debts plus the delivery of deceased animal's skins to the Royal Castle at Newcastle. William would also have been expected to deputise for the sheriff and coroner, effectively as an officer of the Crown. In return for these duties William would have received the use of land, rather than a wage or salary, since payment in ready cash was not always possible at this period.

The Manor of Byker was sold by the Byker family in 1357 and for most of the time between the very early 1400s and 1537 it belonged to the Percy family of Northumberland until confiscated by the Crown for their participation in the religious rebellion against Henry VIII's reforms. In 1543 the Manor was sold by the Crown to James Lawson a prosperous Newcastle merchant-adventurer, alderman and mayor, the descendants of whom continued to own most of Byker for nearly 300 years. During the 1500s the Dent family headed by another affluent Newcastle merchant, is recorded as holding one third of the Manor along with a 'capital messuage' (dwelling house with land attached) plus other tenements, a colliery and a fishery on the Tyne. Byker became part of Newcastle in 1835 and from around this time the sale of land for building plots began.

Originally, Byker was little more than a collection of riverside settlements together with small inland rural communities that included Byker Village and Byker Bar. Change began in 1549 when that part of the Manor facing the river between Ouseburn and St Lawrence Chapel was acquired by Newcastle Corporation for the dumping of unwanted ships' ballast by sailing colliers returning to the Tyne for more coal, for which a charge was made. As a result, this area became known as the Ballast Hills with the money raised benefiting the town.

The first significant manufacturing industry in Byker was glassmaking. In or around 1615, Sir Robert Mansell, a wealthy Elizabethan naval officer, was awarded a royal monopoly to make glass in return for him developing its manufacture using coal-fired kilns rather than timber, which by this time was in short supply. Mansell had selected Tyneside as his preferred location in the country, and the St Lawrence district in particular, because of the abundance of cheap small unsaleable coal, the availability of low-cost raw material arriving as ballast, as well as the river, which gave access to the North Sea and beyond. By

Left: The Tyne and the Byker terraces in 1963. Over the years, much of what is seen here has been totally redeveloped.

the 1730s there were seven glasshouses within a short distance of each other along the riverside at St Lawrence, manufacturing mainly window glass 'which serveth most parts of the Kingdom'. A century later Tyneside had become a major glass producing centre, the industry was second in importance to coal, and Sir Robert Mansell was described as the 'Father of Newcastle Glassmaking'. The St Lawrence glasshouses had all closed before 1900.

With regard to coalmining in Byker, numerous pits were working the High Main seam (and then the deeper Low Main seam) from the early 1700s with collieries based at Lawson Main, St Lawrence and St Anthony's, all connected by wooden waggonways to a riverside staith or quay at St Peters. Initially mining was carried out at no great depth but by around 1800 some shafts were being sunk nearly 800ft below ground level until flooding a few decades later forced coalmining to cease.

Shipbuilding flourished at St Peters from 1756, when William Rowe began what became the Tyne's largest shipyard during the Napoleonic Wars, building not only merchant vessels but also men of war such as the relatively large 970 ton H.M.S. Bucephalus, a 52 gun ship of the line. In 1810 the Smith family (previously rope makers at Byker) developed the shipyard and were noted for their building of East Indiamen sailing ships for the Far East trade. Following Smith's move to North Shields and the founding of Smith's Dock, in 1871 the site was taken over by the marine engineering firm of R & W Hawthorn Leslie who remained for over a century. The modern St Peter's Basin residential development and marina now occupy this former industrial area with some of its names, such as Rowe's Mews, The Ropery and The Moorings, recalling its heritage.

Ropemaking was another important industry in Byker. The Smith family operated the St Lawrence ropery that extended along what is now St Lawrence Road with modern apartment blocks covering the former works.

Further inland, the former Byker ropery has been replaced by industrial workshops alongside St Michael's Road. There was another ropery at St Anthony's; the site is now part of a Riverside Park.

One of the earliest lead manufacturers on Tyneside had their factory in the Ouseburn Valley, first of all beneath what is now landfill and later further downstream where Ouseburn Farm is now situated. For nearly 150 years, from around 1774, until the business transferred to Hebburn, the Ouseburn lead works produced white and red lead primarily for the paint and varnish industry. At St Anthony's another lead factory opened alongside the Tyne in 1846. It became the largest employer in the neighbourhood for a number of years until its closure in 1932. A Riverside Park now covers the site.

Potteries were another significant employer in Byker. From the 1780s they appeared in the Ouseburn Valley, at St Anthony's and a little later at St Peter's. However they had all shut down before 1914 except Maling's two large purpose built factories, known as Ford 'A' and 'B', which soldiered on until 1926 and 1963 respectively.

In addition to these industries there were many other, often smaller, manufacturing concerns operating in Byker, such as iron foundries, chemical works and mills (used for either flax, flint or flour) that have not survived. One of the largest businesses in Byker today is an engineering company, founded in 1922, which more than covers the site of the former pottery and cattle sanatorium at St Peter's.

In 1801, the population of Byker totalled 3,254 and fifty years later it had more than doubled to 7,040 - yet the majority of people lived close to industrial sites at the river's side or Ouseburn leaving the remainder of the suburb largely agricultural and managed by a handful of farmers.

By early 1870s, the medieval manor of Byker had been sold to developers who shortly afterwards began to build homes on a large-scale in the area approximately bounded by Shields Road (north), Allendale Road (east), Walker Road (south) and Byker Bank (west). Most houses were in the style of terraced two storey Tyneside flats with their unique paired front doors (and a similar arrangement at the rear in back lanes) to accommodate one household above another on the same site. Cobbled streets, many with corner shops, were then laid out in a gridiron format often following former field boundaries which sometimes led to steeply sloped thoroughfares.

Byker's population had tripled to 21,011 in 1881 and twenty years later it had more than doubled again to 45,460. In an effort to cope with this population explosion Newcastle Corporation made their first attempt at council housing in 1906 on a two acre site at Walker Road. Population comparisons became more difficult after 1917 when boundary changes split Byker into three administrative districts: Byker, St Lawrence and St Anthonys.

From the 1920s, most of the remaining agricultural land, largely in the St Anthony's district, was transformed by Newcastle Corporation into a substantial area of council housing. Finally during the late 1960s and early 1970s, virtually all the Victorian Tyneside flats, some of which were nearing their centenary, were swept away and replaced by the award-winning Byker Wall estate, quickly followed by the Metro rapid-transit system.

Looking west along Kendal Street, 1950s.

Fossway, Shields Road and Byker Bank

Modern and historic locations shown on the 1895 Ordnance Survey Map (Locations are approximate)

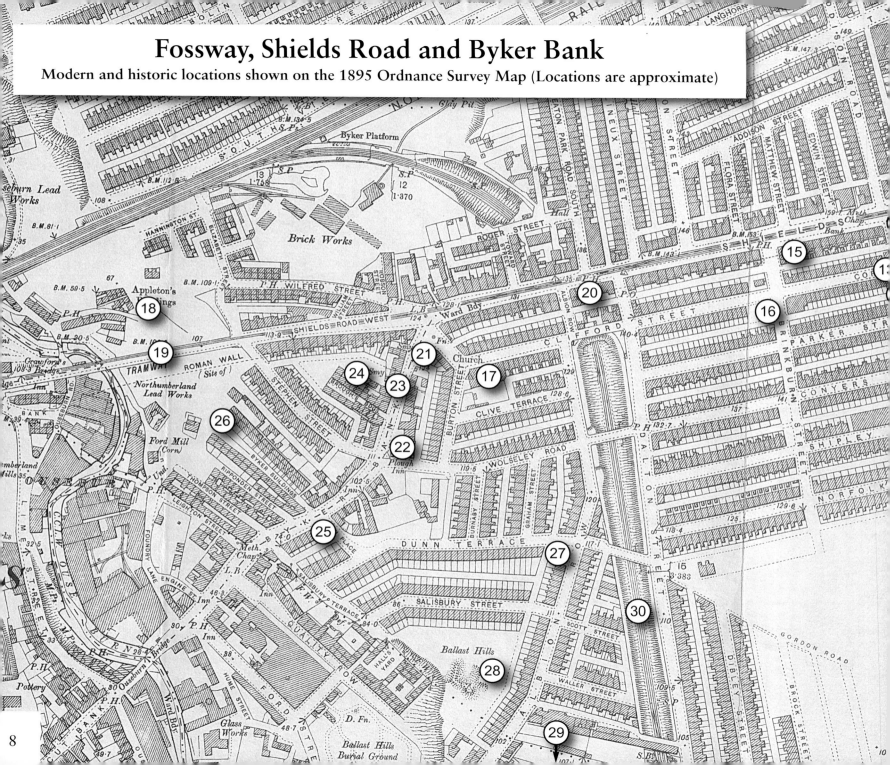

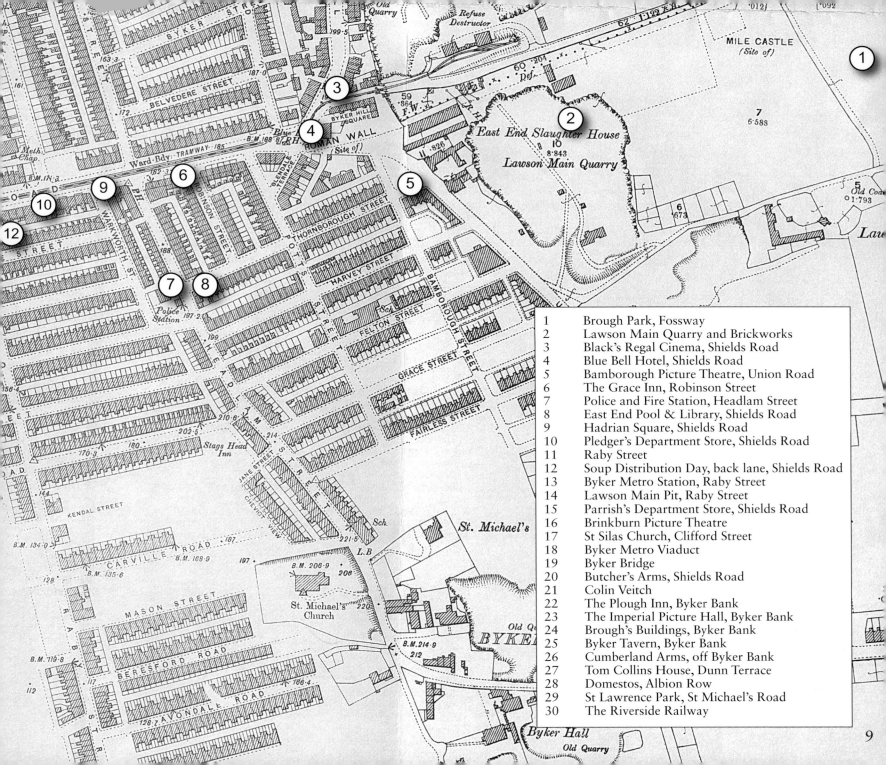

1   Brough Park, Fossway
2   Lawson Main Quarry and Brickworks
3   Black's Regal Cinema, Shields Road
4   Blue Bell Hotel, Shields Road
5   Bamborough Picture Theatre, Union Road
6   The Grace Inn, Robinson Street
7   Police and Fire Station, Headlam Street
8   East End Pool & Library, Shields Road
9   Hadrian Square, Shields Road
10   Pledger's Department Store, Shields Road
11   Raby Street
12   Soup Distribution Day, back lane, Shields Road
13   Byker Metro Station, Raby Street
14   Lawson Main Pit, Raby Street
15   Parrish's Department Store, Shields Road
16   Brinkburn Picture Theatre
17   St Silas Church, Clifford Street
18   Byker Metro Viaduct
19   Byker Bridge
20   Butcher's Arms, Shields Road
21   Colin Veitch
22   The Plough Inn, Byker Bank
23   The Imperial Picture Hall, Byker Bank
24   Brough's Buildings, Byker Bank
25   Byker Tavern, Byker Bank
26   Cumberland Arms, off Byker Bank
27   Tom Collins House, Dunn Terrace
28   Domestos, Albion Row
29   St Lawrence Park, St Michael's Road
30   The Riverside Railway

1. Brough Park, Fossway

Brough Park is situated between the Fossway and Grace Street and was first recorded as a sporting venue in 1917, when a large crowd witnessed a '£40 whippet handicap' promoted by Mr Jack Morrison of the Blue Bell Hotel at nearby Byker Hill. Later that year athletic foot races , such as 'a 60yard handicap dash for £50' spread over 20 heats, were also held at the ground. At this period similar events took place at the Byker Racecourse on Walker Road and at the Victoria Ground at Low Elswick.

Greyhound racing officially began at Brough Park in 1928, when the Newcastle Greyhound Racing Association held their first meeting. This attracted a crowd of around 4,000 people although this was reckoned to be 'less than expected'. The first race over 500 yards was named the Lawson Stakes after the local landowning Lawson family from Brough in North Yorkshire, whose connections with the area inspired the name of the stadium. Greyhound racing continues to be a popular attraction.

A year later Speedway at the stadium was opened by Newcastle's Lord Mayor. The speedway track lies inside the greyhound circuit and is notorious for its long fast straight stretches and tight corners compared with other venues. Named the Newcastle Diamonds the team initially attracted large crowds (around 20,000 on at least one occasion in the mid-1940s) and won league championship titles. Although closed down on a few occasions over the years, largely due to changes in ownership, race meetings remain popular with fans.

Above: *Speedway meeting, 1993*. Right: *From the North Mail, 1929.*

2. Lawson Main Quarry and Brickworks

At over three acres in area and dating from the late 1600s, Lawson Main Quarry was one of the oldest in Northumberland. Its name came from the local landowning family.

Those who have worked the quarry include the Grace family, whose name is remembered in Grace Street at the southern boundary of the quarry site as well as, it is thought, the Grace Inn on nearby Shields Road at the corner of Robinson Street. The site of both the quarry and the adjoining Byker Hill House, where the Grace family lived for many years, is now covered by a superstore, its car park and part of the Byker Hill roundabout.

Stone from the Quarry was reckoned to have been of the highest quality, durable and easily worked without splitting into layers. Some of its uses have included the foundations of the Georgian Tyne Bridge (1781-1876), the Tynemouth Breakwater and the rail viaduct in Newcastle between the High Level Bridge and Manors Station.

Diversification into brick making for local buildings occurred towards the end of the 1800s, when suitable clay could be obtained just a few feet below the surface.

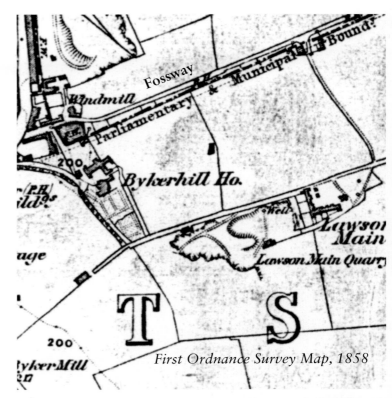

First Ordnance Survey Map, 1858

3. Black's Regal Cinema, Shields Road

Standing prominently on Byker Hill, this white-fronted building with a tall square tower became a familiar landmark, particularly when illuminated at night. Elephant's footprints on the floor guided patrons from the entrance to the pay box and then to the auditorium.

Financed by Alfred Black, this lavishly finished cinema opened in 1934 to seat 1,645 people at costs ranging from 5d to 1/- (afternoon) to 7d to 1/6 in the evening. It was always a popular venue due to competitive pricing

The Rank Organisation took control in 1955 and immediately changed the name to the Odeon. The cinema closed in 1972 and, because a bingo licence was refused, the building operated as a supermarket for a short period. A petrol filling station now covers the site.

Black's Regal Cinema, 1934.

11

4. Blue Bell Hotel, Shields Road

Situated on Byker Hill at the junction of Union Road and Miller's Lane (now the Fossway), this Victorian pub had a commanding view down the length of Shields Road. In the background of this photograph taken in 1897, Glendale Terrace can be seen leading to houses in Potts Street.

Originating from at least 1833, when Anne Stonebank is listed as the victualler, there was a series of different innkeepers at the Blue Bell until, in the early 1920s, it came into the ownership of James Deuchar Ltd. Following various mergers and take overs, the pub closed in 1996. The building is now a cycle shop.

In 2004, part of the Roman Wall infrastructure was discovered adjoining the former pub. It faced the Byker Hill roundabout. The site is marked by a very short length of stone wall, the original width but only one stone high.

5. Bamborough Picture Theatre, Union Road

The Bamboro' as it was usually known, opened its doors in around 1913/1914 on an island site alongside Union Road and bounded on the other sides by Bamborough Street and Thornborough Street. Throughout its existence it was owned by the Renwick family.

Seating capacity increased from 666 at the opening to 750 in 1930. Competition for patrons intensified in 1934 following the opening of Black's Regal only a short distance away.

In 1959 the cinema closed and, following a fire, was demolished six years later . Byker Hill roundabout (above the Metro Tunnel) now covers the cinema site. The adjacent Bamborough and Thornborough Streets no longer exist but their names are remembered in the new development: Bamborough Terrace (alongside Conyers Road) and Thornborough House (Grace Lee Neighbourhood).

The photograph, dated 1963, shows part of Bamborough Street on the right with the spire of St Lawrence RC Church in the background.

6. The Grace Inn, Robinson Street

These premises opened around 1870 as a beer retailing business at 10 Grace Terrace, which at that time was a short section of what later became Shields Road. Two decades later, the building became known as the Grace Inn. It is at about this time Robert Deuchar Ltd appears to have taken control. The present pub at the corner of Shields Road and Robinson Street is a later rebuild.

The pub's name almost certainly refers to a prominent local business family headed by Edward Grace who, as well as being land agent for Newcastle Corporation, was also a civil engineer. He owned the quarries at Byker, had a considerable interest in coal mining and lived nearby at Byker Hill House. This substantial house in its own grounds lay close to the present Byker Hill roundabout and adjoined one of the quarries which was between the Fossway and Grace Street. A superstore and car parks now cover the site of the quarry and house.

Following the death of Edward Grace, the land agency and other businesses were carried on by his nephew, Edward Nathaniel Grace, who also lived for a while at Byker Hill House before moving to Broomfield Tower at South Jesmond. Edward Nathaniel Grace was a local politician and served Newcastle as its Sheriff and Mayor during the 1850s.

7. Police and Fire Station, Headlam Street

Opened in 1903, this building was designed by the well-known Newcastle-based architects, Cackett and Burns Dick.

The photograph shows, from left to right: Fire Station, Clock Tower, Inspector's House and Police Station. There was accommodation for three married firemen on the upper floors of the Fire Station with stabling for three horses and the appliance on the ground floor. Twelve auxiliary firemen lived nearby. The Clock Tower was for the public's benefit at a time when not everyone owned a clock or watch. The Inspector's House came next. Finally the Police Station included sleeping accommodation for twenty single constables on the second floor, each of whom was provided with 'a well fitted cubicle'.

The Fire Station was closed in 1969 and six years later the Police Station moved to Clifford Street. The East End Pool and Library now cover the site.

8. East End Pool & Library, Shields Road

Sir Bobby Robson, the former Newcastle United and England football manager, opened the East End Pool and Library in September 2000.

At a cost of £9million this first-class leisure complex, all under one roof, replaced separate and outdated facilities in the district with the aim of regenerating the area.

The twenty-five metre long main pool has a wave machine to simulate seashore swimming together with a sixty metre flume. However it also has a dividing wall that enables serious swimming to take place at the same time. There is also a twenty metre studio pool with a floating floor that allows the depth of water to vary.

The library has computers, educational videos and talking books as well as lending and reference facilities. There are fitness and dance suites, a crèche and café.

9. Hadrian Square, Shields Road

In the year 2000, work began to provide Newcastle's East End community with an open public square, adjacent to the recently opened pool and library, where people could meet and relax. As part of the development, five shops on Shields Road were demolished and west of Warkworth Street archaeologists revealed foundations of Hadrian's Wall dating back nearly 2000 years.

This discovery reinforced the belief that the seventy-three mile long wall, from Wallsend in the east to the Solway Coast in the west, ran parallel and close to the south side of the present Shields Road, which had been built over the defensive ditch. Archaeologists also discovered further defensive measures in the form of three rows of small pits dug into the space between the wall and the ditch. It is now thought, based on evidence elsewhere in Europe, that each pit contained two large tree branches whose sharpened multi-forked ends interlocked above ground level (a forerunner of barbed wire) to further strengthen an already substantial barrier .

A section of the wall in the square has been preserved to its original width but restricted to the height of a single layer of stone. The position of the three rows of small pits between the wall and the ditch (Shields Road) have been marked with small metal studs.

The illustration below was made in 1725 by a traveller who feared that 'this stately work' (the wall) might sink due to colliery excavations, although 'standing in good order' at the time. This view from near the windmill on Byker Hill towards Newcastle and beyond, clearly shows the ditch to the right (north) of the wall but does not record the vallum which was a prominent defensive feature elsewhere along the wall's south side. It is thought the vallum never existed between Newcastle and Wallsend.

In 1800 it was recorded that a portion of the wall's foundations was removed at Byker Hill 'for the purpose of repairing the highways'. Much worse was to follow as buildings and roads expanded a few decades later. Byker Hill windmill (corn), dating from the early 18th century was gutted by fire in 1866 and its site lies covered beneath a major road roundabout system.

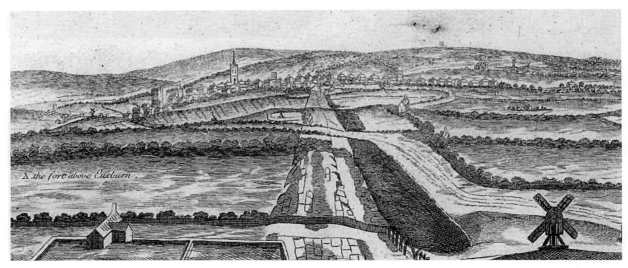

The Wall at Byker, 1725.
Looking west towards
Newcastle, from Byker Hill.

10. Pledger's Department Store, Shields Road

Herbert Pledger (1869 – 1929) arrived from the south of England in around 1893 and opened a drapery business on Shields Road opposite its junction with Heaton Road. As the shop prospered he expanded into adjacent premises that included a former church, once belonging to the United Methodist Free Church and the forerunner of today's Heaton Methodist Church on Heaton Road. Eventually Pledger replaced the properties on Shields Road with a purpose-built distinctive three-storey department store.

The business was successfully continued by the founder's sons until trading conditions deteriorated in the 1950s. After being managed for a short while by nearby Parrish's, the store closed in the early 1960s and today an amusement arcade occupies the building.

Well known throughout the drapery trade in the north, Pledger was also one of the local businessmen involved in the formation of the Sun Ray Clinic in Brinkburn Street, where his wife laid one of the foundation stones (still visible) in 1926.

Advert from the Newcastle Journal, *1953.*

Right: Byker scenes clockwise from top left.
1) *A shop somewhere on Raby Street, 1905.*
2) *Another unknown location in Byker, the sign above the door reads 'Davidson, Licensed Pawnbroker.'*
3) *Headlam Street, 1961.*
4) *Shields Road, late 70s.*

17

11. Raby Street

A view from around 1974 at the top end of Raby Street looking towards Shields Road and beyond to Addison Road, where modern developments were taking place. The imposing three-storey corner building, formerly a branch of Martin's Bank, has fortunately survived. In earlier days a policeman would have been at this busy road junction controlling traffic into and out of Raby Street.

The Raby Hotel on the opposite corner dates from the late 1870s, a time when Shields Road was becoming a major route following the opening of Byker Road Bridge in 1878. Around 1900 the pub was bought at auction by Robert Deuchar Ltd and continues to operate.

Following redevelopment, Raby Street is no longer a busy shopping street and major thoroughfare. It has been truncated close to this viewpoint by a pedestrianised area with a few modern shops leading to Byker Metro Station and beyond into the Byker Wall complex.

12. Soup Distribution Day, back lane, Shields Road

Soup Distribution Days for the needy appear to have been a feature of life in Byker around the early 20th century and perhaps also at other times. This 1903 photograph taken at the rear of the Raby Hotel highlights a crowd of mainly children with jugs waiting to be served with soup and supervised by a stern looking gentleman on the left and two policemen at the back.

The tall building in the background is the United Methodist Free Church on Shields Road, later to be replaced by Pledger's department store.

From Northern Gossip, 1903.

13. Byker Metro Station, Raby Street

Byker Metro Station and the Metro viaduct over the Ouseburn Valley were opened by a local councillor in 1982 as part of the St James' to Tynemouth section of the UK's first rapid transit system, known as the Metro. Three sections had already opened, beginning in 1980, and another three were to follow in 1984, 1991 and 2002.

Most of the Metro system made use of existing railway tracks and stations but on this section expensive civil engineering work was required including a viaduct over the Ouseburn Valley, new stations at Byker and Chillingham Road as well as tunnelling between these stations under Byker Hill.

Initial plans for a motorway between Shields Road and the recently built Byker Wall needed amendment once the route of the new Metro line had been decided. The motorway was then downgraded to a bypass (opened 1990) thus enabling the Metro track to slot into the space provided.

This photograph taken around 1978 illustrates the deep trench needed to accommodate both the Metro track and the bypass. Conyers Road lies immediately behind the excavations with the Shipley Rise part of the Byker Wall dominating the background.

14. Lawson Main Pit, Raby Street

Situated near the entrance to today's Byker Metro Station, the first reference to this pit as a part of the Lawson Main Colliery dates from around 1738 when coal for local consumption was being extracted at 'no great depth' from the High Main Seam. About twenty years later the shaft was sunk to a greater depth of around 450ft, in order to reach the lower part of the seam during the ownership of Matthew Ridley of Heaton Hall.

In about 1800, following the exhaustion of the High Main Seam, a shaft was sunk to the Low Main Seam to a depth of nearly 800ft. Coal mining at this depth was now fully dependant for drainage on the pumping engine at the Friar's Goose colliery on the other side of the Tyne, to cope with the problem of flooding experienced by collieries in the Tyne Basin area.

Once the Friar's Goose pumping engine ceased working in 1851, the Lawson Main colliery and its associated pits were forced to close. Within two decades all trace of this pit at the top end of what became Raby Street had vanished beneath a huge housing development. The only reminders today of this coal mining activity are The High Main popular restaurant on nearby Shields Road and at Saltmeadows in Gateshead where some remains of the pumping engine house have been preserved.

Below left: *The 1858 Ordnance Survey map shows Lawson Main Pit. The star shows the approximate location of the pit.*
Below right: *The popular restaurant on Shields Road is named after the High Main seam.*

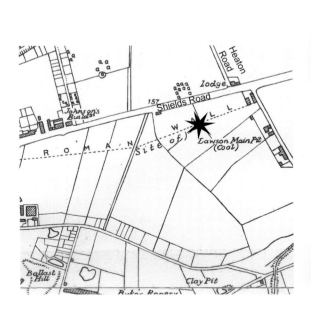

15. Parrish's Department Store, Shields Road

John Thomas Parrish (1850-1908), born in Lincolnshire, arrived in 1874 to set up a small draper's shop at the lower end of Shields Road. As his business grew, he moved to larger premises higher up the road. Following a major fire in 1919 a 'palatial' new store was opened in 1922 although the façade records the year 1921 along with the firm's initials of J.T.P Ltd.

With over an acre of floor space this new ferro-concrete building (to lessen the risk of fire) consisted of three floors plus a basement and was reckoned to sell everything from a packet of pins to a houseful of furniture. The shopping slogan for Shields Road at this time was 'Come East and Pay Least'. A top floor was added in 1934.

A feature of trading at Parrish's was the issue of token money, the equivalent of today's loyalty cards. Periodically a dividend, which varied in value from 1d upwards, based on a customer's spend was declared but it was always paid in circular metal tokens rather than cash. Any change due to a customer was also returned in tokens, and to convert tokens back into cash was expensive.

The store closed in 1984 and this large building, now known as Parrish Court is mainly used as accommodation for students.

The aerial view dated 1964 features the store in the foreground alongside Shields Road with Brinkburn Street stretching away to the top of the photograph. On the opposite corner to the store is the Heaton Hotel (still there) then further along Brinkburn Street the Salvation Army Hall and the Brinkburn Picture Theatre can be seen. Brinkburn Street no longer exists in this format and all the rows of terraced houses have disappeared due to redevelopment.

16. Brinkburn Picture Theatre, Brinkburn Street

Known locally as the 'Brinky', this cinema opened in around 1910. It sat 922 in its stalls and circle with standing places for another 40. In addition to silent films it was usual to include variety acts in the programme. Cycles, prams and go-carts could be stored without charge and Boy Scouts in uniform were admitted free on some weeknights.

In 1930 talking films were introduced which resulted in seat prices being raised to between 6d and 11d. This new technology also meant redundancy for the author's father who had been a resident musician during the days of silent films.

Individual seating replaced benches (suitably padded) in 1937, the consequences of which were that audience capacity had to be reduced by nearly 300.

Following the bombing of the nearby Apollo cinema on Shields Road during the Second World War, the Brinkburn saw increased attendances. However after the Apollo's re-opening in 1956 the Brinkburn suffered a decline in popularity that resulted in its closure in 1960.

Brinkburn Street and its buildings no longer exist in their original form and a modern building, the local Job Centre, now covers the cinema site.

17. St Silas Church, Clifford Street

The Maling family of pottery manufacturers were very much involved in the creation of the new parish of St Silas. Initially, in 1876 , a temporary iron church that sat two hundred was opened at Heaton Park Road South. Later, St Silas Parish Hall was built on this site, which is currently in use as a commercial warehouse.

Nine years later a Miss Maling laid the foundation stone of a permanent new church across Shields Road in Clifford Street, Byker. Designed in the late Gothic style by R.J. Johnson, the Diocesan Architect, this simple but spacious building to seat 660 opened in 1886 with Newcastle's first bishop, E.R. Wilberforce, celebrating Holy Communion. Bishop Wilberforce was the grandson of the anti-slavery campaigner. Unusually this consecration service had to be held in the evening rather than the morning because so many of the parishioners were working people.

A decade later an enthusiastic vicar envisaged St Silas becoming a 'sort of East End Cathedral', and so large were the congregations that complaints arose about the amount of time spent queuing to leave the building.

The situation is very different today. Although surrounding houses have all disappeared, the church remains active, though on a much reduced scale with a charitable business occupying part of the premises. In addition, a moveable glass partition in the church enables social functions to take place without the need for a separate parish hall.

This 1912 photograph highlights the west end of the church including its octagonal bell turret from near the top of Byker Bank, with Clifford Street branching off to the left and Burton Street continuing round to the right. Street patterns have all changed with car parks and a fast food outlet now dominating the immediate vicinity. One of the few changes to the exterior of the church is that the bell turret has been reduced in height and the weather vane removed.

18. Byker Metro Viaduct

At around half a mile long this spectacular viaduct, with its graceful alignment, opened in 1982 to carry the Metro rail line from St James' to Tynemouth over the steep-sided Ouseburn Valley and up into Byker Metro Station.

Designed by international consulting engineers Ove Arup & Partners and taking three years to build (by John Mowlem & Co Ltd), this viaduct became the first in the UK to be erected using a new method of construction consisting of pre-cast segments of reinforced concrete, each weighing around forty tons, glued together with epoxy resin . Afterwards the rail track was laid on concrete slabs over the horizontal segments.

Sir Ove Arup (1895 – 1988) of Scandinavian descent and founder of the consultancy business was born, as well as spending the first few years of his life, nearby in Heaton. Apart from his involvement in other Metro projects, including three stations, several bridges and the award-winning viaduct, he is probably best known as consultant for the Sydney Opera House in Australia.

25

19. Byker Bridge

In 1873, the Byker Bridge Company was formed by a group of local businessmen to finance the cost of building a high level road bridge over the steep Ouseburn Valley to improve access between Newcastle and its expanding east end. The idea of a bridge had been debated in various committees for many years without any progress being made. The Act of Parliament authorising construction received Royal Assent during the following year.

The bridge opened in 1878 for pedestrians only, followed a year later by horses, carts and carriages. All users were charged a toll (1/2d for pedestrians with higher rates for other users) as a means of recovering the construction cost of £82,500 initially borne by the Byker Bridge Company. Horse-drawn trams began using the bridge in 1887 (single track only), again subject to a toll.

This substantial multi-arched bridge built with piers of solid brick (not rubble infill) stood 95ft above the Ouseburn and had a 30ft wide deck, just sufficient for a road and a single footpath.

No sooner had the bridge opened than public agitation began for the tolls to end, which then raised the question as to how the Byker Bridge Company would be financially compensated. After nearly ten years of conflict and court cases, Newcastle Corporation was eventually obliged to meet the cost plus financial adjustments and in 1895 the bridge was declared free of tolls.

In 1902 the bridge was widened by cantilevering footpaths from either side of the roadway, and strengthened to allow electric trams (now with two tracks) to use the bridge. The bridge deck was completely rebuilt in 1985 with crash barriers at a cost of over one million pounds.

Left: *An 1894 sketch of Byker Bridge.*
Next page, clockwise from top left:
1) *Trams and the well-dressed cross Byker Bridge in 1905.* 2) *Three boys play in the smoke and steam of the Ouseburn Valley, 1950s.* 3) *Beneath the bridge in 1972, the area is soon to be developed as Byker Farm, 'Cluny Whisky' can be seen in the background.* 4) *A view of Byker Bridge in 1968 towards the Shieldfield multi-storey flats, beyond the bus on the bridge.*

20. Butcher's Arms, Shields Road

In the early 1870s Edward Dodds moved his butcher's shop and grocer's business the short distance from the top of Byker Bank to new premises at the corner of Oswald Terrace (now part of Shields Road) and Dalton Street. A few years later, Dodds was recorded as a beer retailer and around 1879 the Butcher's Arms Inn was mentioned for the first time together with a butcher's shop in adjacent premises. The 1881 census revealed that Dodd's nineteen year old son John was also a butcher.

The pub was extended in 1890 by new owners John Duncan & Co, wine and spirit merchants with branches in the region, until around 1900 when James Deuchar Ltd took control. At this time the pub was said to be 'one of the best patronised and one of the best conducted in the city'.

Interestingly, in the early 1930s the long established local firm of regional butchers known as R.A. Dodds Ltd took over the premises adjoining the pub and remained for many years. It is unknown whether there was a family connection with the earlier business.

The Butcher's Arms continues to occupy the corner site with Dalton Street, although the adjoining building on Shields Road is no longer a butcher's shop.

Corner of Dalton Street and Shields Road, 1996.

Looking towards Newcastle from outside Parrish's department store on Shields Road near the junction with Brinkburn Street, 1978. 29

21. Colin Veitch (1881 - 1938)

International footballer, musician, actor, playwright, journalist and politician.

The youngest son of a Relieving Officer (who supervised relief to the poor), Colin Veitch was born and grew up on Byker Bank near to its junction with Shields Road, an area now completely altered and replaced with car parks, a by-pass and a fast food outlet.

At 18, Veitch signed on as a professional footballer with Newcastle United at 15/- (75p) per week and then progressed to become a leading player and captain during most of the club's glory days before the First World War. In this successful period the club won three First Division titles, one F.A. Cup and played in another four F.A. Cup finals. Regarded as a versatile midfielder for both club and England, Veitch also earned the distinction of being able to play in almost every position on the field except goalkeeper and in sixteen seasons he made 322 appearances for Newcastle United and scored forty-nine goals.

A founder member of the Football Players' Union, he later served as its chairman for several years until retiring from football and becoming involved in the 1914-1918 war as an army officer.

Away from football Veitch and his family were deeply interested in the performing arts. He was a regular actor at what became the Peoples Theatre in Newcastle, often in the evening after a Saturday afternoon game, and regarded George Bernard Shaw as a close friend. Music was another passion and, apart from composing melodies for pantomime, he was an experienced member of the Newcastle Operatic Society as well as a conductor of the Newcastle Clarion Choir.

A wall plaque has recently been unveiled outside his later home at 1 Stratford Villas in Heaton.

22. The Plough Inn, Byker Bank

Dating from at least the 1820s, The Plough Inn was one of only a handful of pubs in Byker at that time and one of the first on Byker Bank. Situated at the top of the bank, almost alongside the toll bar, it later became one of eight pubs in the short distance of around 400 yards between Ouseburn Bridge (at the bottom) and Shields Road (at the top). A similar number of drinking establishments existed on Cut Bank at the other side of Ouseburn Bridge.

Probably built as a pair of terraced dwellings that became a pub, they were then gradually altered and modernised over the years by new owners, which sometimes resulted in a change of name. In use today as a restaurant, the premises remain as the last of the pub sites on either Byker Bank or Cut Bank.

1996. Beyond the Metro viaduct is the 1930s Apollo Cinema on Shields Road now replaced by a supermarket.

23. The Imperial Picture Hall, Byker Bank

The Minerva Picture Hall was described in 1910 as "the prettiest theatre in the district" when it opened at the top of Byker Bank at its corner with Windsor Street but was relatively small in size with seating for only 360. The name changed in 1918 to the Imperial Picture Hall.

Seat prices during these early days varied between 2d and 9d with 1d off in exchange for three jam jars. The silent movie programme operated twice nightly along with a three-piece orchestra that provided the necessary sound effects and interval entertainment. At Saturday matinees a spotlight would randomly focus on a youngster who would then win a prize. Police charity shows on Sundays were also held during this period when money raised was used by the police to provide boots for barefoot children. In the early 1960s a former usherette remembers some patrons who brought sandwiches and remained all evening to save coal and lighting at home.

The Imperial closed in 1963, largely due to the reopening of the nearby Apollo cinema on Shields Road and the emerging popularity of television. A warehouse occupied the premises for a number of years until it was demolished in 1985 in preparation for new roads that now cover the site.

PROPRIETOR—
J. H. DAWE.

Private Address—
29, North View, Heaton,
Newcastle.

Twice Nightly.

MANAGER
SYDNEY DAWE

Telephone 840 Central

6-50——8-50

Advert for the Imperial, 1925.

24. Brough's Buildings, Byker Bank

Brough's Buildings near the top of Byker Bank and close to its junction with Shields Road West were described in 1827 as 'a neat row of houses erected in 1790' almost certainly for local coal miners. The buildings consisted of fourteen two-storey dwellings lining a short, narrow street where sixty-eight people lived in 1841. The Lawson family of Brough, in North Yorkshire, were land owners in this part of Byker, and where nearby Lawson Street was named after them. Today the site of Brough's Buildings is beneath the busy road connecting Byker Bank with the recent Shields Road bypass and Lawson Street has also vanished completely.

The photographs were taken around 1935, immediately before demolition of the properties. Almost the full length of the street is visible on the upper view near the end of which, on the left, are the outside toilets, which are shown in more detail on the second photo. Note the water tap and barrel (extreme left) and the apparently patient gentleman perhaps waiting his turn.

In 1841 most heads of households were colliers though other occupations included a horse keeper, a grocer and a cooper. Thirty years later 193 people were packed into these fourteen dwellings, presumably now divided into tenements, and residents included a tinplate worker, a driller at the ironworks and labourers – but no colliers. The author's grandfather, the son of a shipwright, spent some of his childhood here.

At the end of the street and partly on Byker Bank stood the Bay Horse Inn that appears to have opened as a beer house around 1830 and become one of several pubs in the vicinity.

Brough's Buildings, 1935.

25. Byker Tavern, Byker Bank

Further down Byker Bank was the Byker Tavern, a pub dating from around the 1860s and known locally as the 'Police Bar' as a result of having being managed by a former policeman. Byker Bank had been a major route between Newcastle and North Shields, as well as a toll road, before the opening of Byker Road Bridge in 1878.

This photograph, taken around 1920 indicates the pub's position on Byker Bank (right) at the corner with Dunn Place (left). On Victorian maps this area is known as Dunn's Buildings and for most of the 1870s a Ralph Dunn was landlord. It is also known that around the 1840s Lawson Dunn owned the nearby Byker Ropery along with its buildings and ground.

Following closure of the Byker Tavern in 1970, its site in the new Byker Wall redevelopment became known as Northumberland Terrace within the surrounding area called Dunn Terrace.

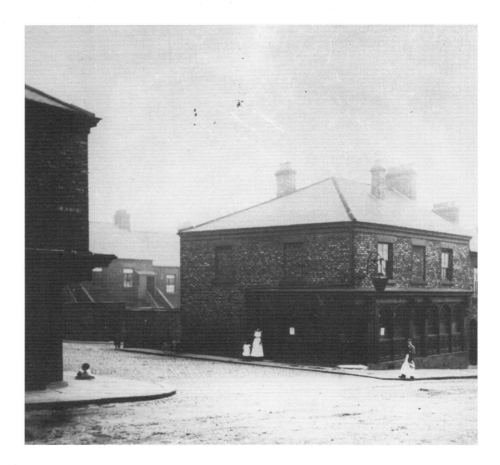

26. Cumberland Arms, off Byker Bank

The Cumberland Arms began as a private house at the end of a terrace of brick dwellings known as Byker Buildings that branched off the steep, busy shopping thoroughfare of Byker Bank. Probably built around 1800, this row of houses is clearly marked on a map dated thirty years later. Sometime after the Beerhouse Act (1830) which effectively allowed any ratepayer to sell beer on his own premises without the need for a magistrate's licence, this dwelling became a beer shop and eventually the Cumberland Arms.

The building collapsed in 1898 during alterations to convert the ground floor into "a more attractive style of bar", which sadly cost the life of a worker. The rebuild was completed during the following year.

One of the most celebrated owners was Jocker Wood (1854 – 1937) an ex-world champion at quoits as well as an all-round sportsman who enjoyed pigeon racing, golf and cycling (including a ride from John O'Groats to Lands' End). He also owned the Masons Arms in Quality Row together with the Duke of York in nearby Back Maling Street.

Today the Cumberland Arms is the sole survivor of the former terrace known as Byker Buildings and continues to be a popular Free House in an area awaiting redevelopment. Above the pub's entrance is a plaque to the memory of Jocker Wood.

27. Tom Collins House, Dunn Terrace

One of the last functions of Councillor Tom Collins as Lord Mayor of Newcastle in 1978 was to open the thirteen-storey wedge-shaped block of flats for older residents in the Dunn Terrace area of Byker, with lift access to all floors.

Named after him, they provide sheltered accommodation in thirty-nine two-person flats tapering from six flats at ground level to only one at the top. There is a call system that links each flat to a resident warden and the building contains other rooms for social activities.

Left: *The Cumberland Arms, 1966.* Above: *Tom Collins House, 2016.*

28. Domestos, Albion Row

The many households that use Domestos as a disinfectant and bleach probably do not realise that the product originated on Tyneside.

In 1929 Wilfred Handley, an ex-dental technician, and his wife began to make the product at their chemical works at the mouth of the Ouseburn using as its main component a by-product obtained from ICI at Billingham. Initially sold in large brown stoneware jars, refills were made by salesmen travelling from door to door on bicycle carts specially adapted to carry the liquid.

The name Domestos is said to derive from *domus* (Latin for a house) and *osteon* (Greek for a bone) – in short 'the backbone of the house'.

The Domestos company was formed in 1936 and around four years later the business moved to nearby Albion Row in Byker into larger premises vacated by College Sweets.

Diversification occurred during the Second World War, largely due to the scarcity and rationing of soap because of a worldwide shortage of fats and oils. Soapless detergents then emerged that used petroleum as a raw material which included Stergene, and some years later Squeezy. Domestos also pioneered the introduction of the soft plastic bottle for washing-up liquid.

With a workforce of around 300 at its peak, Domestos was taken over by Unilever in around 1961 and in 1974 the business was transferred to Warrington due to a lack of space at Byker for expansion. A motor vehicle repair business now occupies the Albion Row site.

29. St Lawrence Park, St Michael's Road

St Lawrence Park opened as a recreation ground around 1908 on the site of the former St Lawrence Brickworks and Clay Pit. Situated between St Michael's Road and Walker Road and immediately to the west of the now disused Riverside Railway, the land had been originally acquired by Newcastle Corporation in the mid-16th century specifically for the depositing of unwanted ships' ballast, and for many decades was part of a much larger area known as East Ballast Hills.

Today the Park consists of several acres of open grassland and scattered trees on a gentle slope, part of which is a children's play area.

St Lawrence Park, 2016.

Advert for Domestos, 1961.

30. The Riverside Railway

The Riverside Railway opened in 1879 as an alternative to the existing and more direct route between Newcastle and North Shields, which lay too far to the north for the increasing number of riverside industrial workers. This new railway branched off the main line at the eastern end of the Ouseburn Rail Viaduct and re-joined it six and a half miles later near Percy Main. Expensive to build because of tunnels, bridges, lengthy cuttings and retaining walls there were also seven 'unpretentious' stations to be built including Byker, St Peter's and St Anthony's.

Byker, the last of the stations to open in 1901 and the first to close in 1954, was actually in Heaton but could not be given that name because of an earlier Heaton Station close by on the main line. Byker station and track now lie beneath the car park of a nearby supermarket.

From here the line entered a tunnel below the Shields Road area and continued towards the river in a long cutting between Dalton Street and Albion Row, which has now been converted into a public walkway known as 'Byker Link, St. Lawrence's Park'. Maling's Ford B pottery, which abutted the railway, made use of it by constructing a siding into their factory.

The line's rather limited time tables were geared to worker's shift patterns, either early or late, and, as a result, the railway never fulfilled expectations even after electrification in 1904 and the later introduction of diesel traction. Apparently stations were frequently closed and padlocked for large parts of the day.

Final closure came in 1973, after which stations were demolished and the double track removed. Much of the line has now been transformed into a public walk and cycleway.

The junction of the Riverside Railway. This slightly blurred image may have been taken from a moving train. The signal box can be seen to the left of the photograph, the tall building to the right of the centre, with the two chimneys is Beavan's departmental store. (Photo: A.E. Young)

The Byker Wall Estate

Modern and historic locations shown on the 1913 Ordnance Survey Map (Locations are approximate)

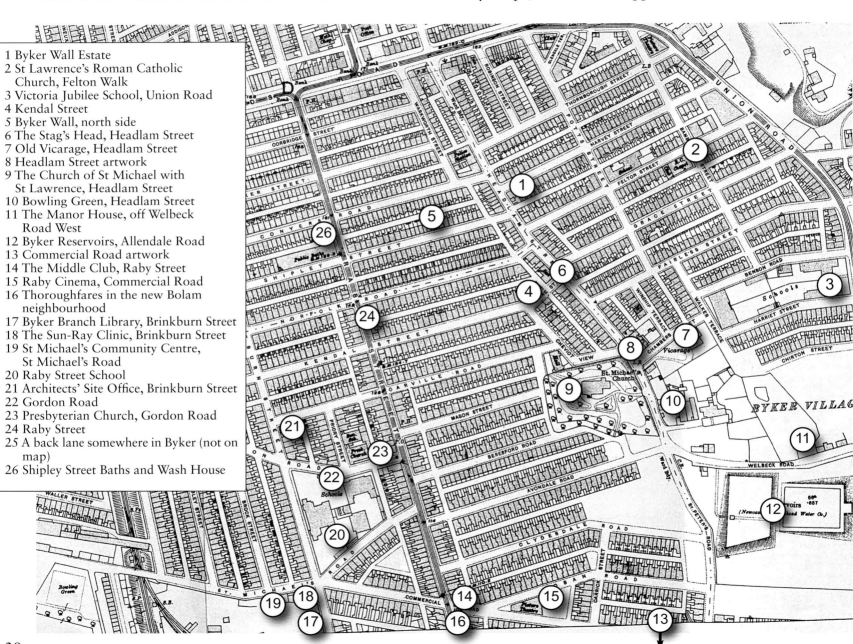

1 Byker Wall Estate
2 St Lawrence's Roman Catholic Church, Felton Walk
3 Victoria Jubilee School, Union Road
4 Kendal Street
5 Byker Wall, north side
6 The Stag's Head, Headlam Street
7 Old Vicarage, Headlam Street
8 Headlam Street artwork
9 The Church of St Michael with St Lawrence, Headlam Street
10 Bowling Green, Headlam Street
11 The Manor House, off Welbeck Road West
12 Byker Reservoirs, Allendale Road
13 Commercial Road artwork
14 The Middle Club, Raby Street
15 Raby Cinema, Commercial Road
16 Thoroughfares in the new Bolam neighbourhood
17 Byker Branch Library, Brinkburn Street
18 The Sun-Ray Clinic, Brinkburn Street
19 St Michael's Community Centre, St Michael's Road
20 Raby Street School
21 Architects' Site Office, Brinkburn Street
22 Gordon Road
23 Presbyterian Church, Gordon Road
24 Raby Street
25 A back lane somewhere in Byker (not on map)
26 Shipley Street Baths and Wash House

1. Byker Wall Estate

In 1960, the area of Byker bounded by Shields Road, Union Road, Walker Road and Byker Bank was scheduled for redevelopment to replace old and overcrowded Tyneside flats that lacked basic amenities. A few years later, property immediately south of Shields Road began to be demolished to create space for a multi-lane motorway. These plans were subsequently amended in favour of the new Metro line and station (opened 1982) plus a two-lane bypass for motor vehicles (opened 1990).

In 1969 Ralph Erskine (1914 – 2005) a London-born architect was appointed to mastermind the development plan. His thirty-year Swedish experience, which included the protection of buildings from Arctic winds, and, in more recent times, his successful housing designs at Killingworth Township had attracted positive attention. Erskine's task was to accommodate several thousand people on a south facing slope and to take into account some important recommendations. These included the need to avoid a gridiron layout of streets, a requirement to separate people from traffic, to retain original amenity buildings if possible and finally to listen to the community. Erskine once remarked "lose the people and it just won't be Byker anymore". It was decided next that roughly half of the people would be housed in a high perimeter wall, primarily for childless residents, and the other half in low-rise dwellings in the shadow of the wall.

The perimeter wall construction began in 1971. At nearly one mile long and up to eight storeys high (mostly five storeys) this fortress-like, serpentine structure curved out to allow residents to be near public transport and shops and curved in to allow car parking space outside the wall. The north side of the wall facing Shields Road was designed to be a barrier against motorway noise and fumes as well as cold northerly winds. As a result, this side is built almost entirely of brick, with intensified patterns near entry points along with tiny windows suitably soundproofed for bathrooms and kitchens. All other rooms face south. Also visible on this side of the wall are the brightly coloured acoustic baffle boxes that conceal extractor fans. The blue shark fin structures on the blue corrugated metal shallow pitched roofs contain the lift motors.

In contrast to the austere north face of the wall, the inner sheltered south side features the doors, large windows, brightly coloured balconies and small gardens. Two-storey family maisonettes are at ground floor level with flats above for childless residents. There is lift access to all floors and the wall is pierced with several entry points, some for pedestrians only and others for vehicles.

Work on the remainder of the area to be rebuilt, south of the wall, began around 1972 and involved the construction of an informal mix of one, two and three-storey low-rise dwellings, some in terraces and others in up to four-storey blocks. Built largely of brick and timber (often brightly coloured) most have shallow pitched corrugated metal roofs, also in a range of colours. There are small courtyards, long and short terraces, play areas for children, scattered trees, shrubs and grassed areas together with random sculpture rescued from some of Newcastle's former distinguished 19th century buildings such as the Royal Arcade, Old Town Hall and YMCA.

The whole area of around 210 acres is divided up into ten zones with names such as Avondale, Ayton and Bolam that reflect former thoroughfares and was largely complete by 1981 when government cut backs forced the scheme to be abandoned. Nevertheless international recognition was obtained with visits by eminent architects and housing specialists, which led to listed status being granted in 2007 to secure its ultimate protection.

Above: *An aerial view of the Byker Wall redevelopment looking north towards Newcastle and the Town Moor (top of photo), 1978 (Tyne & Wear Archives & Museums). Top right: From a 1970s publicity magazine. Bottom right: A 1970s view inside the multi-storey, south-facing wall highlighting balconies, windows and doors.*

Next page, clockwise from top left 1) *Byker Wall with Headlam Street Police Station in the background, 1973.* 2) *One of the many interconnecting internal footpaths in the residential area, 1970s.* 3) *Children play in one of the purpose built family play areas.* 4) *Shipley Street Baths can be seen on the left, 1974.* 5) *A mural of a hot air balloon on the gable end of a building, children play in a pile of sand, 1976.*

2. St Lawrence's Roman Catholic Church, Felton Walk

The present church in Felton Walk, photographed here in 1987, had previously served as the Trinity Presbyterian Church at New Bridge Street for around fifty years. Bought 'very cheaply' by the Dominicans, this church, designed by John Dobson, was then re-assembled stone by stone at the corner of Felton Street and Bamborough Street close to their earlier church and school and opened in 1897. Due to cramped conditions at Byker, the church's original transepts and one of its twin towers could not be rebuilt.

The earlier church and school (in Felton Street) had opened in 1883 on land purchased from Sir John Lawson of Brough, initially to accommodate up to 450 children. As part of the Byker redevelopment in 1973 the Victorian buildings were replaced by a new school nearby at the corner of Spires Lane and Headlam Street.

Byker's first Roman Catholic church had opened in 1877 when the Dominicans took over a disused Methodist chapel near the Mushroom ferry boat landing and named it after the ruins of the nearby medieval chapel of St Lawrence. Sunday services were held upstairs while a school for up to 150 pupils operated on the ground floor.

3. Victoria Jubilee School, Union Road

The Victoria Jubilee School opened in the summer of 1887 as a celebration of Victoria's fifty years as Queen. Performing the opening ceremony was Alderman (later Sir) William Haswell Stephenson, a local industrialist, a generous benefactor to Newcastle and a prominent local politician who served as its Mayor/Lord Mayor on seven occasions.

Fronting Union Road, the school stretched back between Benson Road and Harriet Street as far as Walker Terrace. Today the area is covered by low-rise housing that includes Benson Place, Harriet Place, Jubilee Terrace and Old Vicarage Walk. The double-storey school buildings cost just over £11,000 and were designed for around 1,000 pupils in a total of eleven classrooms plus two halls. Subjects taught included reading, writing and arithmetic, tables, notation and dictation, for which the initial weekly cost per child ranged from 2d to 4d.

The senior boys' part of the school closed in 1950 followed seventeen years later by the senior girls' section, leaving only the younger pupils until the Byker redevelopment resulted in the demolition of the school buildings. A section of the railings have survived on Union Road.

This photograph taken in 1968 is a view of the school from Harriet Street towards the rear of the main block that faced Union Road.

4. Kendal Street

Looking down the steep Kendal Street in 1975 towards Raby Street at its foot from the junction with Jane Street. Beyond Raby Street, new developments can be seen stretching towards the lower Ouseburn valley and beyond to Newcastle.

   This area has now completely changed. All these homes have been replaced with low-rise dwellings and some landscaping with names such as Cheviot Mount and Carville Rise.

5. Byker Wall, north side

The north side of the Byker Wall now has some open green spaces and trees (right) in contrast to the area under development shown below which is rather bleak.
(Photo: K. Bladen 1972)

45

6. The Stag's Head, Headlam Street

The Stag's Head is now the sole survivor of Byker's original pubs within the Byker Wall housing area. First mentioned around the late 1860s as a beer house in Byker Lane (renamed Headlam Street) it belonged to Edward Pickering who then continued as landlord for the next forty-six years. Following his death, the Pickering family continued to run the pub for a further twenty-four years until Robert Deuchar Ltd bought the business in 1938 for £19,500. For many years, and for obvious reasons, the pub was also known locally as Pickerings.

The photograph, dated 1974, features the pub at the corner of Headlam Street and Jane Street before an upgrade to the building. Part of the Byker Wall is visible to the right.

Originally a four storey windmill (corn), known for many years as Heron's Mill, had once occupied this site at the junction of the 'lane to Byker' (Headlam Street) with the nine acre 'Jane Field'.

7. Old Vicarage, Headlam Street

Completed in 1870 for the sum of £1,400 it was the home of the vicar of Byker until around 1963. From that time it became the headquarters of the local battalion of the Boys' Brigade and known as David Grieve House after Dr David Grieve, a Newcastle GP and a prominent Presbyterian layman, who was deeply interested in the Boys' Brigade movement.

The building has now been converted into apartments.

8. Headlam Street artwork

Under the roof of an ornamental gateway to St Lawrence's RC School in Headlam Street are 4 pieces of decorative ironwork each in the shape of a 6 pointed Star of David. These items were recovered from Heaton Railway Station following its closure in 1980 and originated as brackets at the top of cast iron columns that supported the platform roof.

Parts of these wrought iron gates, which partially restrict vehicle access to Headlam Street, were salvaged from Jesmond Manor House at the time of its demolition in 1929 and probably date from the 18th century. The pieces from Jesmond are the two narrow panels standing fore and aft of the main gate structure, plus the panels on the other side of Headlam Street (not pictured here).

9. The Church of St Michael with St Lawrence, Headlam Street

At one of the highest points in Newcastle, previously occupied by the Byker Folly, the Bishop of Durham consecrated the new parish church of St Michael in 1862. The Byker Folly, which had replaced an earlier windmill, was described as "an artificial castellated ruin" erected on land owned by the Ridley family in 1713 and regarded by them as a pleasing object to be seen from their residence at Heaton Hall.

The new parish of Byker had been created out of Newcastle's All Saints parish to meet a large increase in the East End's population. The Ridleys donated the land together with permission to use the stone from a neighbouring quarry. Mr W.L. Moffatt of Edinburgh, as architect, designed the building in the Decorated style to seat 490 at the remarkably small cost of £2,500.

In 1936 the church was considerably extended to seat nearly 750 worshippers, with material recycled from the recently demolished St Peter's Church in Ellison Place Newcastle. Among the additions were a complete north aisle, vestries and the doubling in length of the chancel. An organ also came from St Peter's along with the organist who it is reported could play while holding a cigarette concealed under one hand.

From 1979, the church became known as St Michael with St Lawrence following the demolition of the St Lawrence Church of England building on Walker Road and the consequential merger of both parishes.

Although the church is, at the time of writing, undergoing extensive restoration, regular weekly services continue to be held. Outside the church in the Byker Garden, which opened in 2011, superb views towards Newcastle and Gateshead can be seen together with a direction indicator plinth and pavement tiles recording some of Byker's eventful past.

The Church in 1910.

Top: *A postcard of Byker Bridge, 1904.*
Below: *A view towards Newcastle from the Byker Wall, 1975.*

This page, clockwise from top left.
1) *Looking up Raby Street to the new Byker Wall, 1975 (Dr Tom Yellowley)*. 2) *Looking down Raby Street, 1975 - Atkins Chemists with clock on the right*. 3) *The top of Raby Street, 1970.*

Next Page: *An aerial view of Byker and Heaton, 1970. In the bottom right of the photograph the Byker Road Bridge and Ouseburn Rail Viaduct can be seen. The centre of Byker is in a transitional stage, many of the terraces have been demolished, although many buildings such a St Silas Church and Parrish's department store were spared the wrecking ball at that time. Part of the Riverside Railway is visible in the centre of the picture, leaving the main line.*

Clockwise from top left.
1) *Catching up with the gossip on Shields Road at the junction with Grafton Street.* 2) *Seven Stories now occupies the former flour warehouse at 30 Lime Street.* 3) *The bridges behind Byker City Farm, 2007.*

Byker from the air, 1986. *The Byker Wall Estate dominates the upper part of the image with the fortress-like wall enclosing the low-rise dwellings. The Metro line and station can be seen, but the bypass has not yet been constructed. The Police Station on Clifford Street is present, and the route of the old Riverside Railway is clearly visible.*

V

JOCKER WOOD
MASONS ARMS.
QUALITY ROW, QUSEBURN, NEWCASTLE.

Both pages, clockwise from top left: 1) *The congregation of St Lawrence Church, 1958.* 2) *Men pose in front of trophies won for quoits, pigeon flying, bagatelle, cycling and golf. Jocker Wood sits in the front front, second from right, Mason's Arms, Quality Row.* 3) *Another aerial photograph of taken during the construction of the Shields Road bypass in 1986.* 4) *'Climb Newcastle' was opened in 2008 in the old swimming pool building which was closed twenty years previously.* 5) *A recent photograph of the inner face of the Byker Wall.*

VII

Washing day in a Byker back lane, 1970s.

10. Bowling Green, Headlam Street

Major plans in the 1960s to redevelop Byker with modern housing unfortunately led to the demise of Byker Park and, in particular, to the potential loss of the popular bowling green. However, a successful petition saved the bowling green, which continues to be a valuable amenity in the neighbourhood.

Byker Park originated in 1926 as a result of Newcastle City Council's determination to replace 'open space' lost at Castle Leazes, because of extensions to the Royal Victoria Infirmary, with land in suburbs such as Byker in need of further recreational facilities. The park was situated between Headlam Street and Bothal Street approximately on the site of what had been Byker Village and its adjacent quarry. At around five acres in size, the park consisted of a children's play area, some gymnastic apparatus, four tarmacadam tennis courts and a bowling green. The project was estimated to have cost £12,000 and provided half a year's work for about fifty men at a time of high unemployment.

Today this area is known as Chirton and is covered with modern housing with names such as Chirton Wynd, Manor House Close and Headlam Green. On the other side of Headlam Street, opposite the bowling green, is the former St Michael's Church Hall, built in 1928 'by the voluntary offerings of the parishioners with the aid of charitable benefactors'. The building now houses the Byker Community Association.

A game in progress, 2016.

11. The Manor House, off Welbeck Road West

Although the Manor of Byker is frequently mentioned in historical records of the early Middle Ages there are no references to the Manor House. However by 1500 Roger Dent is recorded as holding 'two messuages (a dwelling house with outbuildings and land) and 200 acres in Byker' and it seems probable that the Manor House may well have once belonged to this Newcastle merchant and former mayor of the town. A century later the Dents were described as 'holding a third of the Manor of Byker plus a coal mine and fishery'. Although the Lawson family of Brough became major landowners in Byker it is not thought they ever lived at the Manor House.

The former Manor House had become the Blue Bell pub some time before 1825 and is described at this time as having 'gabled ends, mullioned windows, a stone porch, heavy lintelled doors and thick defensible walls'. Inside it is said that its quaint old rooms that once contained many fine oak carvings (subsequently used as firewood!) retained several pieces of 'curious tapestry' albeit in a mutilated condition. The building was demolished in 1863.

The Manor House stood in Byker Village on what is now the north side of Welbeck Road, near its junction with Headlam Street. Today the site is covered by the Manor House Close residential development.

The Manor House in the 17th Century.

12. Byker Reservoirs, Allendale Road

In 1898, high ground at Byker was purchased to build three reservoirs to serve the expanding east end of Newcastle. Two reservoirs had been completed six years later at a cost of nearly £47,000. One of these reservoirs was built of brick, had a roof and was designed to contain three million gallons of filtered water for domestic consumption while the other was an open masonry tank to store unfiltered water for commercial use. The third reservoir, another open masonry tank, was never built.

Difficulties soon arose regarding the filling of the reservoirs and in fact they were never used. Much of the problem appears to have centred on a recently built bridge of pipes across the Ouseburn that needed to be removed because of impending major redevelopment at that part of the Quayside. In 1908 some of the redundant pipework (still visible) was recycled into the new low-level road bridge at the mouth of the Ouseburn that replaced the 17th century packhorse bridge leading to the glasshouses.

The redundant reservoirs were demolished in 1968 and two years later the Newcastle and Gateshead Water Company opened their new headquarters building on the same site, bringing together different departments under one roof. Following the departure of the Water Company several years ago, the premises, between Allendale Road and St Peter's Road, are now occupied by Newcastle City Council's Neighbourhood Services Department.

The photograph below dated 1902 features part of the reservoirs under construction.

13. Commercial Road artwork

On the south side of Commercial Road near its junction with St Peter's Road is a brick archway giving pedestrian access into the Ayton Rise district. The inner side of this archway reveals a stone doorway with columns supporting a pediment between two small arches, said to have been recovered during the demolition of Elswick Hall, Newcastle, around 1980.

Elswick Hall, designed and built in the very early 1800s, was for a short time the home of Richard Grainger the entrepreneur behind the development of Newcastle's town centre in the 1830s.

14. The Middle Club, Raby Street

The Byker and St Peter's Social Club reopened in 1978 at the corner of Raby Street and Commercial Road after nearly two years of extensive alterations at a cost of over £250,000. Huge improvements included a complete rebuild of the concert room with a stage that could be seen by all, as well as the modernisation of the lounge and bar. One of the most popular performers at the club was Tyneside comedian Bobby Thompson known as 'The Little Waster'.

In order to distinguish this club from St Peter's Social Club, further down Raby Street at its junction with Walker Road, the former became known as the 'Middle Club and the latter as the 'Bottom Club'.

15. Raby Cinema, Commercial Road

The Raby was one of the city's earliest cinemas, when it opened around 1910. Situated on a triangular plot of ground at the junction of Commercial Road and Oban Road, some locals knew it as the 'Coffin', because of its shape, while others referred to it as the 'Pie and Gravy'.

Originally the whole of the downstairs was fitted out with long wooden forms, where you were told to 'shove up a bit' until someone fell off the end. The problem with silent films was reading the subtitles and as your head 'moves like a pendulum' patrons were frequently heard asking 'what does it say'. Audience participation seems to have been an accepted part of the cinema experience, including 'screaming at the baddies', 'cheering at the goodies' together with the ducking of heads as guns were fired. A three-piece orchestra provided the sound effects and the musical entertainment.

Between films there were variety acts including magicians, who usually had to endure whistling, shouting and being told loudly how tricks were done. There were lantern slides advertising local businesses: 'Steeles – Fish and Chips 2d' ' Elwell – Your jovial barber, shaving 3d'.

Talking films arrived in 1930, at which time total seating capacity was 823 (pit 450, stalls 195, circle 178). Although the cinema was not wide enough to adopt new technology, the Raby continued successfully until the coming of colour television which eventually forced its closure in 1959.

Two years later the building re-opened as a bingo club. The photograph shows it in 1977, just a few years before it finally closed, with Oban Road on the left and Commercial Road on the right. Following demolition in 1989, the site is now unrecognisable due to new roads and modern housing, though Commercial Road remains as a bus route.

16. Thoroughfares in the new Bolam neighbourhood area

In most of Byker's new neighbourhood areas earlier street names were retained as much as possible to identify new thoroughfares and walkways. However, in the new neighbourhood areas of Ayton and Bolam, a naming problem arose because some of the long streets of old Byker (principally Ayton Street and Bolam Street) passed through both of the new areas.

In order to avoid confusion by adopting similar street names in each of the new neighbourhood areas, it was decided that a set of additional names was needed for the Bolam area. The subjects chosen were the names of birds in dialect form, taken from poetry written by Thomas Doubleday (1790-1870) a local poet, soap manufacturer and political agitator. They were: Cushat Close (wood-pigeon), Houlet Garth (owl), Laverock Court (lark), Merle Gardens (blackbird), and Ruddock Square (robin).

17. Byker Branch Library, Brinkburn Street

This library opened at Brinkburn Street in 1940 and there is a plaque inside the building recording the date. A great deal of discussion about the suitability of the site had taken place beforehand, particularly because of its relative isolation near the edge of a densely populated area. The site had formally been part of Maling's Pottery Works (Ford B) and the plans were to build a similar library to the one recently opened at Fenham in 1938.

In the year 2000, Byker Branch Library was superseded by the new East End Library near Shields Road. The former library building, photographed here in 1967, is now an industrial workshop.

18. The Sun-Ray Clinic, Brinkburn Street

Byker Sun-Ray Clinic at the corner of Brinkburn Street and St Michael's Road was opened by Lord Armstrong in 1928. Regarded at the time as one of the best designed and equipped buildings of its kind in the country, it was founded to assist those suffering from rickets, tuberculosis and skin diseases, with the benefit of ultraviolet radiation as a way back to health. Around 350 patients were expected to be treated each day.

The final cost was anticipated at around £6000 and a novel way of raising the necessary finance was to offer, in return for a donation of one guinea (£1.05), the donor's initials to be inscribed on the dado inside the new building. It is thought Sir James Spence an eminent paediatrician and Professor of Child Health at the University of Durham was the driving force behind the clinic's establishment. When he requested £40 to buy the first sun ray lamp, it is on record that a 'storm of protest erupted'.

Six foundation stones (still visible outside the premises) were laid two years earlier by some of the wives of local businessmen, including Lady Parsons, who it was felt had more in common with children and young people. It was then expected that local businessmen would continue to fund the project.

In the early 1990s the clinic's community health services were moved elsewhere in Byker to make them more convenient for local residents. The building now appears to be in use as an industrial workshop. Set into the brickwork near the entrance to this single storey building is an attractive stone plaque showing a colourful radiant sun together with the words The Sun-Ray Clinic.

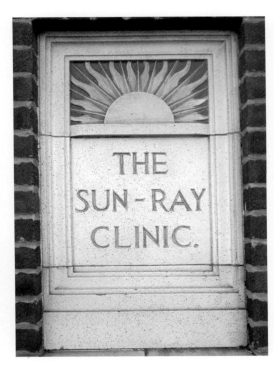

19. St Michael's Community Centre, St Michael's Road

In 1924, Mrs Myles Beavan, wife of the department store owner, laid the foundation stone (still visible) of this building in St Michael's Road on land previously part of Maling's Ford B pottery. Intended to be an up-to-date clubroom for the Young Women's Christian Association (YWCA.) it comprised a large hall, two classrooms, and a kitchen large enough for cookery classes, a bathroom and a secretary's office.

When opened it replaced two separate clubrooms in Newcastle's East End with the aim of saving money. Most of the cost of the new building, estimated at around £3000, was expected to be raised from a 'big bazaar' at Newcastle's Barras Bridge Assembly Rooms.

Byker Mission eventually took over the building and was succeeded by the St Michael's Community Centre with facilities for a youth club, keep fit sessions, martial arts classes and discos. An industrial workshop now occupies the premises.

20. Raby Street School

Raby Street School opened in 1897 on what had been 'a fine open site' of nearly two acres between Raby Street and Brinkburn Street. The Mayor of Newcastle led the ceremony. The well-known Newcastle architect, William Lister Newcombe, designed the buildings to accommodate nearly 1,400 children, ranging from infants to seniors, at a cost of nearly £16,000.

During the first week, records show that 555 infants were admitted, many of whom had never had any previous schooling, to be 'taught' by only four teachers supported by two pupil teachers. Infants were 'packed like sardines' into raised galleries with desks that were 'too shaky' and positioned too close together for adequate supervision. In the junior school it was common for classes to consist of over sixty pupils. It is thought the frequent low attendance levels caused by infectious diseases and poor weather must have been a welcome relief to otherwise harassed staff.

Much of the Victorian school was demolished in the mid-1970s and replaced with new buildings, extensions to original structures and other improvements such as additional play areas, a nursery unit and up-to-date facilities. Now called Byker Primary School, it was designed for 320 pupils. Officially opened in 1977, the new school cost almost £300, 000. The former school gymnasium was converted into a much-needed Youth Centre at an additional cost.

The photograph at the top shows the school in the early 1970s, probably taken from St Michaels Road. The photograph on the right, taken in 1967, shows part of the school building that was demolished several years later.

21. Architects' Site Office, Brinkburn Street

A former undertaker's premises in Brinkburn Street (at the corner with Carville Road) was taken over by Ralph Erskine in 1969 as a site office for his team of architects some of whom 'lived over the shop'. For the next 15 years it served not only as an office but also as a 'drop in' centre for residents to enable them to be consulted at all stages during the development.

Following completion of the development, the building was taken over in 1987 by the Byker Community Housing Service, which continues to deal with residential matters.

A plaque on the outside wall (now very difficult to read) commemorates the work of Ralph Erskine as a 'humane and inspirational architect' and features a balloon that apparently appeared on all of his sketches as a symbol of optimism and freedom. Ralph Erskine CBE died 2005 aged ninety-one.

Below: *At their office, the architects consulted with residents and kept them informed of progress. Children had a say in what they'd like to see in play areas.*
Below left: *Part of a concept drawing from Ralph Erskine's office.*

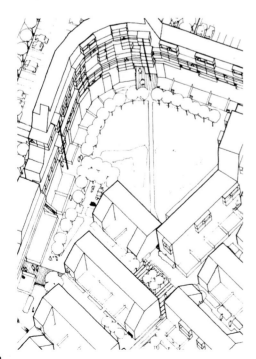

22. Gordon Road

Road sweepers pose for the camera at Gordon Road in 1910 with part of Raby Street School visible on the right. All these buildings have now been demolished.

Occupying this site today is a small-tree lined square surrounded partly by modern housing, the Byker Primary Pre-School Centre and the Victorian and former Presbyterian Church (hidden from view on this old photograph by 19th century housing on the left).

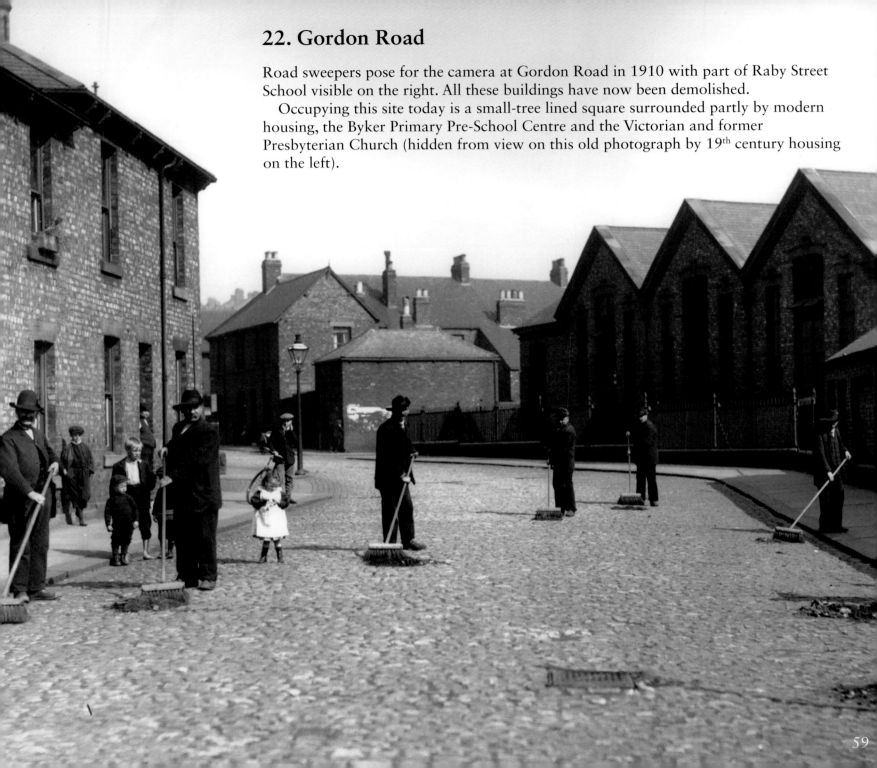

23. Presbyterian Church, Gordon Road

Byker Presbyterian Church opened in Gordon Road in 1897 and was the first to be built under a scheme of the Synod (which had met in Newcastle the previous year) to build churches 'in large working class districts'. Its foundation stone had been laid by Mr Henry Robson of London, a liberal supporter of the Church's schemes. Designed in the simple Early Gothic style by Newcastle architects Badenoch and Bruce, its seating capacity was 750, including 270 in the galleries.

Six years later a new hall (to seat 500) plus classroom facilities and a caretaker's house were added alongside the church. The same architects were engaged.

Following its closure as a church, a proposal in 1999 to convert the building into a counselling clinic with dormitories for victims of family breakdown and abuse met with fierce opposition from local residents. Their successful appeal against the clinic was based on the fact that there was a primary school less than 100 yards from the church.

The church (now used as offices) and the façade of the adjacent hall survive amid modern developments.

24. Raby Street

On the next page: Originally, around half a mile in length and one of the longest thoroughfares in Byker, this view looks down Raby Street towards Walker Road on a sunny day in around 1970. On the left is Kendal Street with a Co-op shop on its corner with Raby Street.

Raby Street has completely changed with all these buildings having been replaced by mainly low-rise dwellings on either side of a narrow 'access only' thoroughfare. Different colour schemes are a feature of the modern housing with predominantly blue paintwork in upper Raby Street while further down the street red and green prevail.

61

25. A back lane somewhere in Byker

Much of old Byker consisted of long parallel streets of Tyneside flats with many of them running in an east to west direction and stretching down from the Byker Hill area.

This photograph, dating to around 1974, illustrates a typical back lane that served two streets but remains so far unidentified. Back lanes were popular with children for games and with housewives on washdays – that is until the coalman or the bin man arrived.

Some of the coal hatches can be seen between pairs of doors.

Highlighted in this photograph are the back doors to the upper flats. An open staircase led from them into a small yard containing a coal-house. The back door of the lower flat that opened into its own small yard is out of sight behind the wall. Each flat then had a separate door, arranged in pairs, giving access into the back lane from their yard.

26. Shipley Street Baths and Wash House

In 1886, the Mayor of Newcastle opened the new Byker Baths and Wash House in Shipley Street at its corner with Raby Street around thirty-five years after Newcastle's first baths and wash house opened in what later became City Road.

Designed with red bricks in the Gothic style by the local architects Gibson and Milner Allen, the interior of the building contained a swimming pool, since it was "important that boys should learn to swim". Next, there were private individual baths arranged in a gallery around the pool where persons "could make themselves thoroughly clean after a hard day's dirty work". Finally there was the wash house for those living in small houses with no facilities for washing clothes. Each person was allocated a cubicle, complete with a drying horse heated by hot air. A patent wringer, worked by a steam engine, was also provided.

'Great satisfaction' with the arrangements was reported and in the first week 1,088 bathers and 112 users of the wash house were recorded, resulting in an income of nearly £12. Later a successful campaign resulted in keeping the baths open later on Friday and

Saturday evenings, 9pm instead of 8pm, to encourage more working men "to take their usual weekly bath".

The buildings were declared "surplus to requirements" by Newcastle City Council in 1993 but because they were by that time an integral part of the Byker Wall they could not be demolished. The former boiler plant in the basement of the wash house became an emergency supply for hundreds of nearby dwellings.

A Climbing Centre now occupies the site of the former pool and at least two gyms operate in the former wash house building.

Shipley Street baths, 1980s.

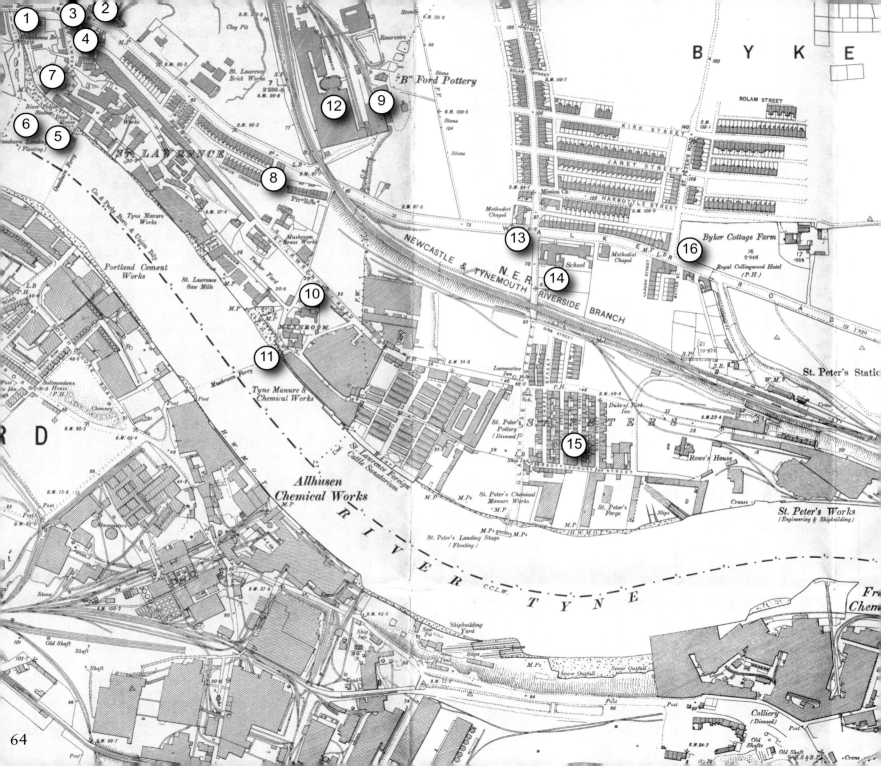

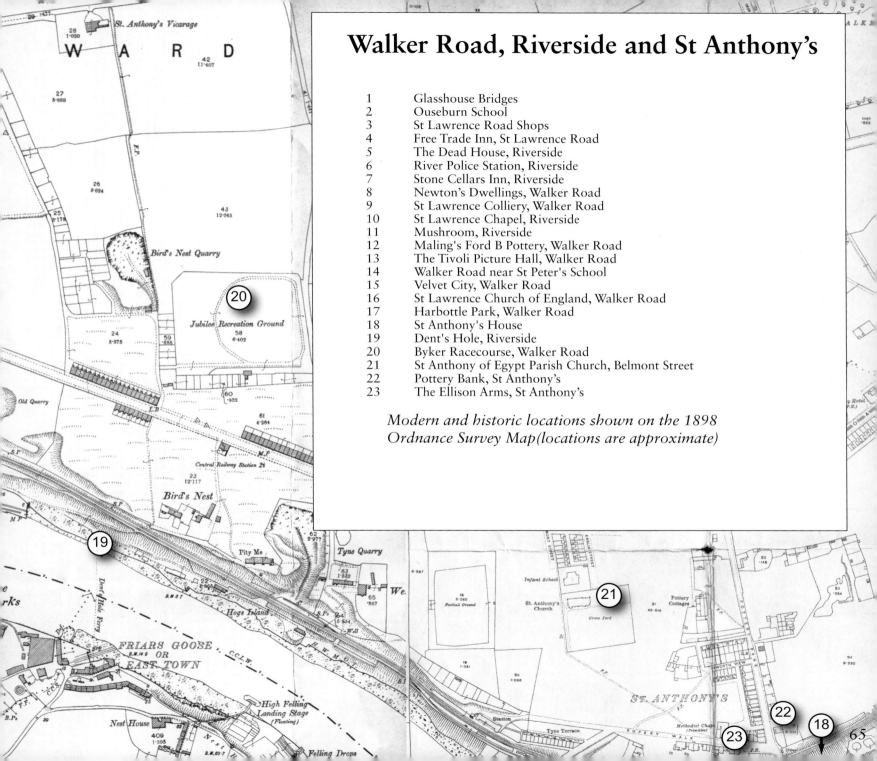

Walker Road, Riverside and St Anthony's

1 Glasshouse Bridges
2 Ouseburn School
3 St Lawrence Road Shops
4 Free Trade Inn, St Lawrence Road
5 The Dead House, Riverside
6 River Police Station, Riverside
7 Stone Cellars Inn, Riverside
8 Newton's Dwellings, Walker Road
9 St Lawrence Colliery, Walker Road
10 St Lawrence Chapel, Riverside
11 Mushroom, Riverside
12 Maling's Ford B Pottery, Walker Road
13 The Tivoli Picture Hall, Walker Road
14 Walker Road near St Peter's School
15 Velvet City, Walker Road
16 St Lawrence Church of England, Walker Road
17 Harbottle Park, Walker Road
18 St Anthony's House
19 Dent's Hole, Riverside
20 Byker Racecourse, Walker Road
21 St Anthony of Egypt Parish Church, Belmont Street
22 Pottery Bank, St Anthony's
23 The Ellison Arms, St Anthony's

*Modern and historic locations shown on the 1898
Ordnance Survey Map(locations are approximate)*

65

1. Glasshouse Bridges

For around three centuries a packhorse bridge, initially built of wood (1609), then of stone (1669) and finally a bridge 'made even and commodious both for horse and foot' (1729) had linked both sides of the Ouseburn during the time that the huge glass industry dominated this area. In 1908, following major quayside improvements the bridge was removed (with gelignite) and replaced by a low-level bridge of steel suitable for vehicles. Incorporated into the new bridge were pipes (one is still visible) installed a few years earlier to carry water over the Ouseburn in order to fill the never-used Byker reservoirs, a short distance away.

The present high-level road bridge over the Ouseburn opened in 1878. Built of brick with five elliptical arches it carried a 26ft roadway plus 7ft wide footpaths on either side around 37ft above the high water level. The bridge cost the net sum of £14,000 after contributions from adjacent property owners - who it was felt would ultimately benefit from this direct route between Newcastle and Walker. At the opening ceremony flags were everywhere, a gun salute was fired and civic dignitaries crossed the bridge to the sound of a police band playing *The Keel Row*. A commemorative stone tablet survives on the bridge parapet.

This 1906 photograph features the high level bridge in the background, the 18th century packhorse bridge at a lower level and one of the reservoir pipes visible in between. To the right are some of the remains of the High Glasshouses buildings, a site now occupied by a modern structure containing a cycle hire business and café.

2. Ouseburn School

Ouseburn School opened in 1893 near the eastern end of the high level Glasshouse Bridge to accommodate 928 children on the ground and first floors. The second and top floor had facilities for cookery, laundry, art and technical workshops because it was felt that there was more to education than pure academic work and in particular 'an urgent need for well-cooked food'.

This attractive and substantial brick built school, with its oriental-style ornate twin towers (part of the building's ventilation system), was designed by the successful Newcastle architect F.W. Rich. In 1960 the school closed and the premises have been occupied by the Quayside Business Development Centre since 1993. The building is now protected with a Grade II official listing.

3. St Lawrence Road Shops

An early 20th century view of buildings near the east end of the high-level Glasshouse Bridge at the junction of St Lawrence Road and Walker Road. Recently developed apartments now occupy the site.

In the foreground is a pair of shops. A provisions dealer occupied the premises to the left, with its shop sign barely legible above the window, while to the right was a confectionery business.

Beyond, at the road corner stood the Rose and Crown pub (closed 1989) with a possible customer waiting for opening time. In the distance is part of Ouseburn School with one of its twin ventilation towers distinctly visible.

4. Free Trade Inn, St Lawrence Road

The Free Trade Inn is thought to have opened on this site around 1850 as a beer house (where a magistrate's licence was not required) in a mixed industrial and residential area. The name may be associated with Britain's policy at that time of moving towards free trade (the abandonment of tariffs, duties and other restrictions on imports) in an attempt to expand the economy and make it the 'workshop of the world'. Situated on high ground (Ballast Hills) overlooking the mouth of the Ouseburn, the pub was surrounded by a hive of industry that included glass and bottle works, an iron foundry, a firebrick factory and a ropery.

It first appears in records in 1881, when the young landlord was described in the census as a 'Beerhouse keeper and Forgeman'. Several years later the pub was rebuilt, and in 1919 Newcastle Breweries took control. A full publican's licence was granted in 1963. Now, a free house, the building overlooks the Tyne with superb views up river towards Newcastle and Gateshead but without the original housing and industry.

This view of the pub in 1913 above the new Quayside extension retaining wall is substantially the same a century later apart from the demolition of the industrial building (upper left) and the removal of the railway lines.

5. The Dead House, Riverside

In the early to mid-19th century, the highly industrialised region near the mouth of the Ouseburn was where a lot of drownings occured (reportedly averaging one a week).

The first recorded mortuary near this area was at the Milk Market end of Sandgate in 1839. Later it moved to a small house next to the Ouseburn Police Station in Tyne Street. Following complaints from local residents, the morgue was again forced to find new premises. In 1873 it settled across the Ouseburn at St Lawrence in a small wooden shed attached to the rear of the Stone Cellars Inn, overlooking the Tyne near to the junction with the Ouseburn. Known locally as the Dead House this shed contained grappling irons, boat hooks and coils of rope and was seldom without a silent occupant. The roof of this low level shed can just be seen immediately below the sign board on the picture taken around 1890.

After the closure of the Inn it appears that the Dead House relocated into the main building.

In the early 1900s all buildings in this area were replaced by the Norway Wharf complete with travelling cranes and transit sheds. Today, much of this riverside location is vacant and awaits redevelopment, apart from a modern style building with a squat square tower near the mouth of the Ouseburn.

Cuckoo Jack, alias John Wilson (1792-1860), the son of a clock-repairer, was a Sandgate waterman who hired out boats for a living. This well-known Tyneside character also had a profitable side-line which involved the recovery of bodies from the Tyne and delivering them to the Dead House in Sandgate. It is estimated that during his life he retrieved around two-hundred corpses, for which the Newcastle Corporation paid him up to 15 shillings (75p) for each cadaver.

As a waterman, he was very familiar with the river's tides, currents, shoals and sandbanks during the years before dredging began in the 1850s. This enabled him to earn additional income by not only hooking up humans, either dead or alive, but also recovering lost property such as watches, bracelets and coins for which he made an appropriate charge. The tools he used included grappling irons, hooks of all kinds and curved forks with fine netting between the prongs.

Following the river's improvement it became a criminal offence to search for lost objects in the Tyne. Undaunted, Cuckoo Jack became assistant to the river's harbour and quay master. This new work entailed supervising the loading and discharging of cargo together with the organisation of boats in tiers along the quay, which sometimes extended halfway across the river.

The Dead House viewed from the river in 1890.

6. River Police Station, Riverside

This illustration, dated 1887, features the River Police Station, adjacent to the Dead House, with its gable end facing the river, 42 years after the establishment of this branch of the Newcastle Police Force. Part of the small low-level shed that served as the mortuary for a number of years can just be spotted beyond the white-fronted building that became the rear of the Stone Cellars Inn. The building to the left of the River Police Station belonged to Robert B Lyon, a manufacturer of patent boiler covers.

In the early 1900s this group of buildings was replaced by the Norway Wharf and today most of this part of the St Lawrence district is vacant and awaits redevelopment.

Top left: *From the* Monthly Chronicle, *1889.*

The west end of the River Police Station looking south-east, 1906, by which time it had extended into the premises of the former manufacturer of patent boiler covers.

7. Stone Cellars Inn, Riverside

This quaint riverside tavern (photograph below), the haunt of many waterside characters, was initially situated behind some old whitewashed riverside dwellings at St Lawrence near the mouth of the Ouseburn. The inn and dwellings probably originated during the 17th century because of their proximity to the surrounding industry and in particular to the glasshouses. In Newcastle's first trade directory (1778) James Henzell, a surname familiar in glassmaking circles, is listed as landlord at 'Glasshouses, North Shore'.

For many years inquests on people who had drowned were carried out by the coroner in a small upstairs room with a low ceiling and oak panelled walls. At some time before or during the 1850s the inn expanded into the adjacent and vacant dwellings and then, following the inn's closure in 1893, the Dead House occupied the empty pub building.

Just before the pub closed, it became the subject of one of Ralph Hedley's important paintings. Titled *Weary Waiting* it portrays a wife carrying a baby and accompanied by a young son waiting at the well-worn steps of the Stone Cellars Inn for her husband, who could be seen through a window drinking with friends.

In the early 1900s, this important riverside area was transformed into the Norway Wharf (some of the metal capstans remain) and a century later much of the site awaits redevelopment.

8. Newton's Dwellings, Walker Road

Newcastle Corporation's first attempt at the provision of council housing was achieved in 1906 when 126 workmen's dwellings were opened on a two-acre site between Walker Road and St Lawrence Road opposite Maling's pottery. Known as Newton's Dwellings, they were dedicated to Henry William Newton who, as an enthusiastic social reformer, had pioneered their development through numerous and often sceptical committee meetings. Although a practising surgeon, he also served the city as an Alderman, Sheriff and twice as Mayor before receiving a knighthood.

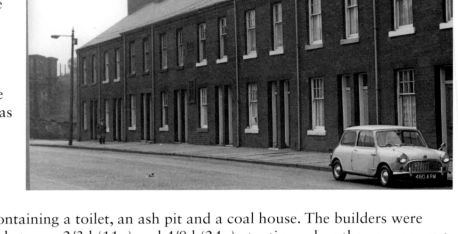

Designed by the City Architect (F.W. Holford) these two-storey flats for those of limited means were predominantly two-roomed although a small number had only a combined living/bedroom. Each dwelling included a scullery (or kitchen) together with a yard containing a toilet, an ash pit and a coal house. The builders were Franklin & Sons Ltd of Jesmond. Weekly rents ranged between 2/3d (11p) and 4/9d (24p) at a time when the very poorest men's weekly wage was approximately £1. A children's playground was also part of the scheme.

The photograph, taken around 1965, highlights a few of the two-roomed terraced dwellings on Walker Road with their distinctive paired front doors. The left hand door led to the ground floor flat while the right hand door accessed the upper floor. To the left of the buildings is part of the bridge masonry of the former Riverside Branch Railway, which today carries a public walk/cycle way over Walker Road. All housing has been replaced in recent times with a light industrial trading estate.

9. St Lawrence Colliery, Walker Road

St Lawrence colliery at East Ballast Hills had two separate periods of mining activity and was linked by a wooden rail track around four-hundred yards long to a riverside staith.

Mining began during the mid-1700s, when for a short period the High Main seam provided a limited supply of coal until flooding forced the mine to close. The second period commenced in 1833 when the colliery re-opened with the sinking of a 550ft deep shaft to reach the Low Main Seam, where the coal was nearly six feet thick and considered 'in great perfection'. By this time the threat of flooding had lessened because of a powerful new pumping engine at Friar's Goose colliery near Gateshead which was capable of draining collieries in the Tyne Coal

Basin including St Lawrence. Part of the Friar's Goose engine house remains as a building of historical interest near Gateshead's International Stadium.

The mine extended under the Tyne and westwards to at least Sandgate but there were problems. At one point a hewer's working space was as little as two feet and in 1834 disaster occurred when a candle caused an explosion resulting in the death of three miners and creating three widows and sixteen fatherless children. Later, the colliery was one of the first to install cages for the lowering and raising of men and ponies as well as for the lifting of coal rather than the hitherto unreliable and dangerous use of the traditional miner's basket.

Following closure of the colliery in the mid-19th century the site was taken over by the Maling family in the late 1870s for their new Ford B pottery.

10. St Lawrence Chapel, Riverside

St Lawrence Chapel, now demolished, stood close to the riverside at Mushroom immediately to the west of the former Spiller's Flour Mill on land now awaiting re-development.

St Lawrence, was probably born in Spain and died in around 258 AD when he was reportedly roasted alive on a grid-iron for diverting the treasures of the church for the benefit of beggars in his care.

Although the first reference to the building occurred in 1340 it is thought the architecture dates from at least a century earlier. The chapel was probably founded by an early Earl of Northumberland *'for the benefit of sick people and wayfaring men in time of need.'*

The chapel closed in 1536 at the time of the Reformation, when no goods, chattels or ornaments were recorded. Annual income of the Chapel was less than £3 and it was agreed that this sum be allocated as a pension for life to the last incumbent.

Visiting the ruined chapel in 1782, local historian John Brand found it in use as a 'lumber room belonging to an adjoining glass house' and local people talked of buried treasure in a vault nearby 'haunted by apparitions'. Forty years later another local historian, Eneas MacKenzie, discovered the chapel being used as a 'ware-room for bottles'.

The last report of the chapel was in 1886 at a time when the St Lawrence Iron Mission Church of England opened at the corner of Raby Street and Harbottle Street.

The Mushroom Hotel, 1886.

11. Mushroom, Riverside

The origin of the name of the riverside district called Mushroom, situated approximately between St Lawrence and St Peters, is unknown. The first recorded reference to Mushroom occurred in 1736 when Henry Bourne, in his *History of Newcastle upon Tyne*, referred to the 'Mushroom Glass-House' as an alternative name for the St Lawrence Glass-House, at that time just one of several glasshouses in the area east of the Ouseburn known as East Ballast Hills.

The Mushroom Hotel appears to have opened in around 1870 and was one of three pubs in this compact and industrialised riverside location. Mushroom was also a landing stage for steamboats linking Newcastle with Shields and as a ferry departure point for Saltmeadows on the south side of the river. The Mushroom Hotel was the last of the three pubs to close in 1903.

The area also featured The Tyne Manure & Chemical Works, which was replaced by Spiller's Flour Mill in 1938. Following the final demolition of the mill and clearance of the site in 2011 the area awaits redevelopment.

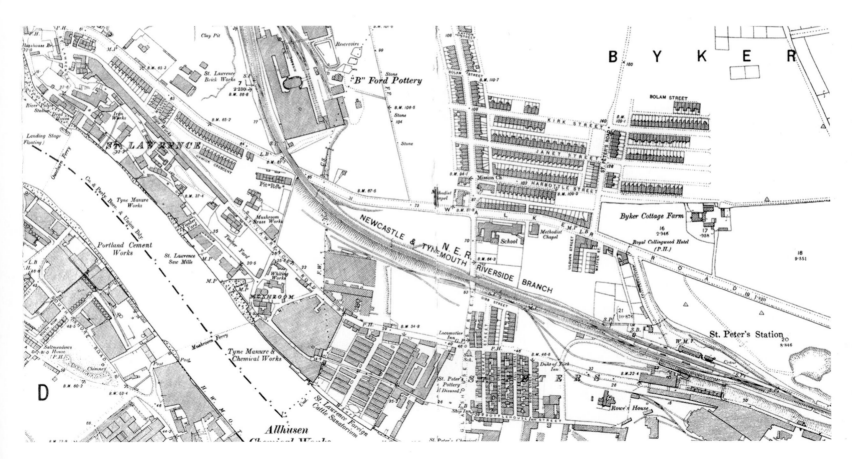

Many features of Mushroom and St Lawrence appeared on the 1898 Ordnance Survey map.

12. Maling's Ford B Pottery, Walker Road

The enthusiasm to manufacture the popular jam pot on an even greater scale prompted Christopher Thompson Maling to build an additional pottery on Walker Road around half a mile east of his earlier factory in the Ouseburn valley. Opened in 1879, this new pottery became known as Ford B to distinguish it from the earlier Ford pottery, now called Ford A. Built on a 14-acre site, where the St Lawrence Colliery once stood, the new pottery was purpose-built and self-sufficient, with dovetailed manufacturing processes to achieve maximum efficiency. That same year, the Riverside Branch Railway line opened adjacent to the pottery, which resulted in sidings being created within the factory.

This new pottery was about twelve times more productive than the earlier Ford A pottery and was thought to be the largest pottery on one site in the UK and possibly in the world. Eventually it had a workforce of at least 1,000, most of whom were women. Working conditions were considered ideal with well-lit ventilated workrooms and the use of leadless glazes. Additionally, there were adequate washrooms, dining rooms and kitchens where employees could cook their own meals. A chapel, school (for children of employees) and allotments were also provided.

At a later date the pottery diversified into products such as scientific, kitchen and dairy equipment, then fashionable decorated tableware, which involved dozens of design patents. In 1908 a new range of breakfast, dinner and tea sets was launched under the trade name of *Cetem Ware* (after C.T. Maling). There was a flourishing export trade too.

Following family bereavements, severe overseas competition and sluggish economic conditions in the UK, the pottery closed in 1963. Now known as Hoult's Yard (named after the local firm of removal and storage contractors who purchased Maling's premises in 1947) most of the former pottery buildings are occupied by small independent businesses.

In 1901 Maling employed around 1,000 workers many of whom were female. Because their shoes were always covered with white clay-dust they became known as 'Maling's White Mice'.

Workers at Maling's preparing pottery for the Coronation of King George VI.

13. The Tivoli Picture Hall, Walker Road

This photograph, taken around 1910, features the Tivoli Picture House which had opened two years earlier in a former Methodist Chapel at the corner of Walker Road (left) and Raby Street (right). At this time a white sheet served as a screen for silent films, which had the disadvantage that whenever a draught blew it revealed the owner's family living room 'sometimes with them eating fish and chips'. Although reckoned to have been the third picture hall opened in Newcastle it had a short life and within four years had closed, probably because it was too near its more successful competitor The Raby higher up Raby Street.

W&R Jacob & Co, biscuit manufacturers, rebuilt much of the area on Walker Road between Brinkburn Street and Raby Street in the mid-1920s and remained for about forty years. A 'By Appointment' stone with heraldic arms remains near an entrance door on Walker Road.

Around 1946 the St Peter's Social Club opened their new premises on the corner site. Known locally as the Bottom Club, as distinct from the Middle Club further up Raby Street, it has an engraved metallic information panel at its main entrance door in Raby Street detailing 'The Legend of St Peters'. Above this door is a large plaque featuring an armour-clad Sir Peter Riddell displaying his family's coat of arms (see photograph).

It is usually thought that the district of St Peter's derived its name from Sir Peter Riddell, a Newcastle hostman, MP and mayor who leased riverside land at East Ballast Hills from Newcastle Corporation in 1630 for a wharf or quay. Then, over time and because of its saintly neighbours (St Lawrence and St Anthony) the name of the area changed from Sir Peter's to St Peter's. However, some local historians contend that St Peter's acquired its name from a chantry or chapel at All Saints Church, Newcastle, dedicated to St Peter and supported financially by income from land at Byker in the early 1400s.

The large plaque above the club's entrance door..

14. Walker Road near St Peter's School

A 1910 view looking east along Walker Road from its junction with Raby Street as road sweepers pose for the camera. None of the buildings remain and Raby Street at this point has been re-named Bolam Way.

The terraced houses on the left have been replaced with an open landscaped area and, in the distance, the St Lawrence Church of England building has given way to modern housing. Some of the houses nearest the camera, built in the early 1870s, formed a short terrace known as Stanley Street on an otherwise empty and recently formed Walker Road. It was around here at that time the Stanley Cricket Club began, followed a few years later by the Stanley Football Club. The Football Club prospered and moved to more convenient sites in the locality before changing its name to the East End Football Club and then finally settling at St James's Park in 1892 as Newcastle United.

On the extreme right of the photograph is part of the St Peter's Board School, which opened in 1876 as a mixed school for infants as well as older boys and girls. Accommodation was for 1,044 children in ten classrooms, plus three assembly halls all heated by hot water pipes and, for those children travelling from a distance, 'gas heated plates were available to warm their dinners'. The school closed just over a century later to make way for a waste disposal incinerator that provides heating for the Byker re-development. As one former pupil commented 'I suppose the old, friendly school and the new incinerator both supply their own type of warmth'. Next to the school along Walker Road (centre of photograph) was the Methodist Brown Memorial Church that existed until the 1940s.

15. Velvet City, Walker Road

Velvet City was the colourful name given to the group of humble mid-nineteenth century dwellings known as St Peter's Village, situated between Walker Road and the River Tyne. Nobody seems to know how the name of Velvet City came about but the people who lived in this relatively isolated and close-knit community thought of it as marvellous, friendly and a place where there was always something happening, such as 'an accordionist playing in the streets'. This compact village had as many pubs as streets, two Methodist chapels, a school and was surrounded by industries which, at various times, included a pottery, cattle sanatorium, manure factory and a shipyard that later became Hawthorn Leslie's Engine Works.

The photograph of Fell Street (named after Thomas Fell who ran the pottery) illustrates the run-down state of the dwellings a few years before their demolition in the 1930s.

By the 1930s most of the village was run-down, 'usually infested with rats' and the decision was taken to re-house residents in nearby Evistones Gardens. Light industry has now replaced much of the former village. The shipyard and engine works site has been transformed into modern homes and a marina known as St. Peter's Basin.

11 & 13, FELL STREET.

(Fronts of houses)

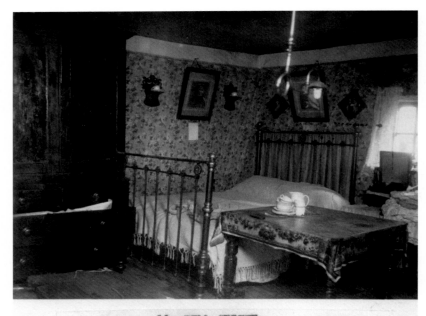

11, FELL STREET.

Interior of room (ground floor back).

Top: *Fell Street, 1929.*
Bottom: *Conditions inside 11 Fell Street, 1929.*

82

16. St Lawrence Church of England, Walker Road

In 1908, when the Bishop of Newcastle blessed this new brick-built church to serve the crowded district of St Peter's, there were so many parishioners trying to attend the consecration service that a large number were disappointed. Nevertheless, the relative large sum of nearly £20 was received in donations and allocated towards the cost of the new building which amounted to £2,746. Apparently, most of this expense was later met by local businessmen 'interested in the spiritual welfare of their employees'.

Situated on Walker Road between St Peter's Road and Till Street, the church was designed to sit 450 in a plain style with narrow round arched windows by local architects Hicks and Charlewood. The photo dates from around 1920.

From 1886, a temporary iron church accommodating 400 had stood at the corner of Raby Street and Harbottle Street. When the new church opened the iron church became the church hall (known locally as 'the shack') until a purpose-built hall opened in 1930 adjoining the church.

Following Byker's redevelopment in the 1970s, congregations dwindled to such an extent that the church, its hall and vicarage closed in 1979 and were then demolished a few years later to make way for modern housing. The parish of St Lawrence then merged with St Michael's Church in central Byker and became known as St Michael's with St Lawrence.

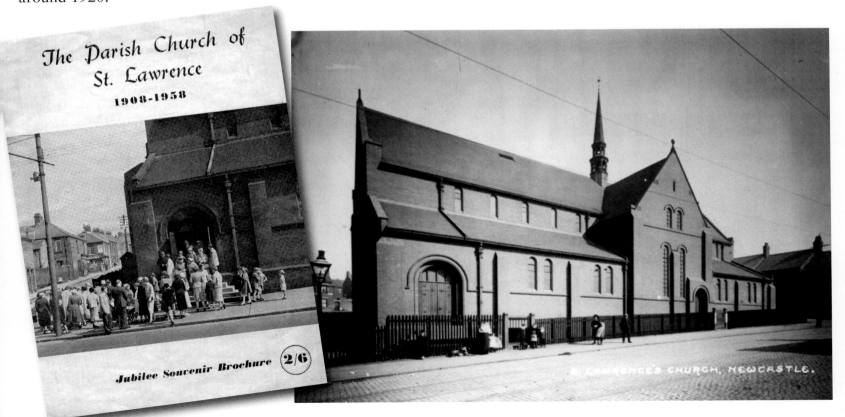

The Parish Church of St. Lawrence 1908-1958

Jubilee Souvenir Brochure 2/6

ST. LAWRENCE'S CHURCH, NEWCASTLE.

17. Harbottle Park, Walker Road

In the mid-1920s nearly twelve acres of land (at £500 an acre) belonging to the former Byker Cottage Farm was acquired by Newcastle City Council to create a recreation ground. The purchase was specifically to offset the loss of open land at Castle Leazes required for the extension to the Royal Victoria Infirmary. A similar transaction resulted in the creation of Byker Park.

Now named Harbottle Park (after Harbottle Street nearby) it fronts Walker Road and Allendale Road and includes a children's play area together with some sculpture.

18. St Anthony's House

Roger Lawson, son and heir of Sir Ralph Lawson of Brough, North Yorkshire, and his wife Dame Dorothy had been living at Heaton Hall with their large family for around nine years when in 1614 Dorothy was suddenly widowed at the age of 34. Her father-in-law was then anxious to sell Heaton Hall and being aware of Dorothy's determination as a devout catholic, to devote the rest of her life to her 13 children, 'religion and good works' suggested that she move to St Anthony's which had the reputation of being a holy place. It was here that a picture of the saint had hung from a tree near the river for many years 'for the benefit and comfort of visiting seamen'.

At this remote location 'more pleasant and private than Heaton' Dorothy had a 'commodious' house built in 1620 which included a chapel. Jesus was inscribed in large letters on the gable end of the building facing the river and Dorothy continued to practise openly as a catholic for the remainder of her life despite severe penalties for doing so. She died in 1632, aged 52.

During the English Civil War this substantial building, known as St Anthony's House was 'razed to the ground' in 1644 by Royalist troops to prevent its use as a

barracks for the invading Scottish army but was later rebuilt and then extended in the next century.

By the mid-1850s the mansion was surrounded by various industries (including a pottery, a ropery, a lead works and a chemical business) which resulted in the building being converted from a private residence into the Ellison Arms Inn run by John Tweddell who had previously been a grocer and spirits dealer in nearby Walker.

The inn had a relatively short life because of the construction of the Riverside Branch Railway which opened in 1879 and passed through the grounds immediately to the north of the main building. In the meantime a new Ellison Arms public house opened at the other side of the rail track in Ropery Walk (now Felling View) near the foot of Pottery Bank

At a later date the former mansion, now known as the Old Hall, operated for several years as a tenement building until its demolition in 1935. The site now forms part of the Riverside Park.

Clockwise from top left: 1) *Pigeon fanciers gather waiting the return of their flock* 2) *Byker lasses in the back lane of Parker Street* 3) *Patrons of the Locomotive Inn, St Peter's, which was demolished after an air raid in 1941* 4) *Byker boys in Kendal Street (Dennis Astridge)*

85

19. Dent's Hole, Riverside

Dent's Hole was a small riverside village between St Peter's and St Anthony's, with one of the few deep water berths on the Tyne during the days of wooden sailing ships. At one time it also served as the normal anchorage for Greenland whalers and similar sized vessels.

Many of its inhabitants would have worked at the nearby St Peter's dock which, during the Napoleonic Wars, was the most important shipyard on the Tyne and where wooden warships would have been launched into deep water. At a later date, East Indiamen, some as much as 1,600 tons, were built and launched from this shipyard. The initial owners of the shipyard were the Rowe family from 1756 followed by the Smiths (later of Smiths' Dock fame), until Hawthorn Leslie & Company took possession in 1871. Today, this area is known as St Peter's Basin and consists of modern residential housing built around a marina with one of the thoroughfares appropriately named Rowe's Mews.

The Dent family, after whom the village was almost certainly named, appeared during the early 16th century in Newcastle as mercers and land speculators. Around a century later they had become influential and wealthy and it is recorded they then owned one third of Byker, including Dent's Hole, a nearby colliery as well as a fishery. Some family members became hostmen and others served Newcastle as sheriffs and mayors.

The drawing from around 1830 by J.W. Carmichael looks up river towards the glasshouses district from near some of Dent's Hole's picturesque old houses. On the left is a wherry, or flat bottomed barge, about to leave the quay.

20. Byker Racecourse, Walker Road

The origins of Byker Racecourse can be traced back to at least 1886 when the advert on the right appeared in the Newcastle Daily Chronicle.

In the 1881 census Robert Smith, described as a fitter and beer retailer, was living with his family at the Bird's Nest Inn Walker Road, which stood in open countryside between old Byker and Walker, except for the industrial riverside area.

Early in 1887 Robert Smith was promoting rabbit coursing, an ancient field sport that involved greyhounds chasing, catching and killing rabbits for the benefit of those wishing to gamble on the outcome. At the same time Smith was also organising handicap races for both greyhounds and athletes, usually for a first prize of £5. These events were held 'within 100 yards' of Smith's home on Walker Road in a six-acre field, which was later named the Jubilee Recreation Ground in celebration of Victoria's fifty years as Queen.

During the summer of 1899 the Jubilee Ground was transformed from a 'wilderness' into a 'New Racecourse for Newcastle' and renamed Byker Racecourse. The enlarged ground (nearly twenty-three acres) had been secured by the promoters on a fourteen-year lease and was now capable of accommodating several thousand spectators who were expected to arrive at this rural venue either by tram, railway, river steamer or on foot. A wooden fence, nearly one mile in circumference, totally enclosed the racecourse and there were four entrances, each provided with a turnstile. The paddock included stables for horses together with rooms for jockeys and the press and nearby, in course of construction, was a grandstand to hold 1,000.

Horse racing on the flat began during the August Bank Holiday weekend with the Heaton Stakes Handicap over one and a quarter miles for £20. The last of the day's six races was the shorter Jesmond Handicap for £15. The Tradesmen's Trotting Handicap over one and a half miles (£25) took place on the following day together with a 120 yard handicap for athletes that required 15 heats before the £25 prize was awarded.

After that summer little or no further horse racing appears to have taken place at the racecourse, which may have been due to the greater popularity of other local venues such as High Gosforth Park. Greyhound racing and rabbit coursing, however, continued to be popular attractions as were athletic events, sports days and flower shows until, in 1920, George Angus & Co Ltd acquired part of the racecourse for a branch of their engineering business. Shortly afterwards, Newcastle City Council began to convert the remainder of the surrounding open fields into a large housing estate. The site of the racecourse today is roughly within the area bordered by Walker Road, Monkchester Road, Birds Nest Road and the section of grassland that now covers the former Bird's Nest Quarry.

Meanwhile at nearby Brough Park, similar events for dogs and athletes began in 1917 and it was here in 1928 that the Newcastle Greyhound Racing Association held their first race meeting.

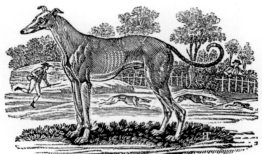

21. St Anthony of Egypt Parish Church, Belmont Street, St Anthony's

Consecrated by the Bishop of Ripon in 1868 to serve the new parish of St Anthony's the church was designed within a limited budget by local architects Austin and Johnson. Newcastle at this time did not have its own bishop. Intended for 360 worshippers the 'neat and commodious' plain church was built with the best quality red bricks rather than the local stone (which discolours quickly in industrial areas) and the building's relatively low cost of £2,300 was largely due to the site having been donated by Sir Walter James, a generous benefactor to Tyneside.

Egypt was added to the church's name at St Anthony's to avoid confusion with the earlier Roman Catholic Church at nearby Walker dedicated to St Anthony of Padua (Italy), who had been a monk in the 13th century. St Anthony of Egypt, on the other hand, was born in Egypt nearly a thousand years earlier and had spent most of his life as a religious hermit.

Byker's association with the saint can be traced back to the Middle Ages when a picture of St Anthony had hung from a riverside tree in this area for the benefit and comfort of visiting seamen. During the 17th century the tradition was continued by Dame Dorothy Lawson (1580-1632) a devout Roman Catholic and one of St Anthony's earliest residents.

The south side of the church as featured on this photograph (c1920) remains virtually unchanged and original plans for a steeple and a north aisle never materialised. Regular church services continue and the former burial ground has been transformed into open grassland following the removal of the memorial stones.

2602. S. ANTHONY'S CHURCH, NEWCASTLE.

22. Pottery Bank, St Anthony's

These 19th century dwellings on Pottery Bank would have originally been home to many of the workers at either the pottery, less than two-hundred yards away up the bank towards Walker Road, or at Locke Blackett's riverside leadworks roughly twice that distance in the opposite direction. Several other smaller industries existed nearby.

On the other side of Pottery Bank from these old dwellings, and out of sight on this mid-1930s photograph, were allotment gardens beyond which lay a new housing estate built during the inter-war years.

Apart from this new housing estate, everything else in this area from the past has been removed leaving a riverside park and some vacant land higher up Pottery Bank awaiting re-development.

23. The Ellison Arms Hotel, St Anthony's

The Ellison Arms Hotel once stood at the foot of Pottery Bank near to its corner with Ropery Walk (now Felling View) and was one of five pubs within a very short distance of each other in a highly industrial area. The pub closed in 1980 to make room for a housing scheme that has since been replaced by an extensive riverside park consisting of open and wooded areas with foot paths and cycleways.

Points of interest on the 1980s photograph include the Riverside Railway viaduct behind the Ellison Arms, part of the housing development in Ropery Walk and the vacant corner site where The Shoulder of Mutton pub once stood.

It is thought the Ellison Arms was named after the ancient merchant family of that name who owned land in various parts of Tyneside and where the name has frequently been commemorated.

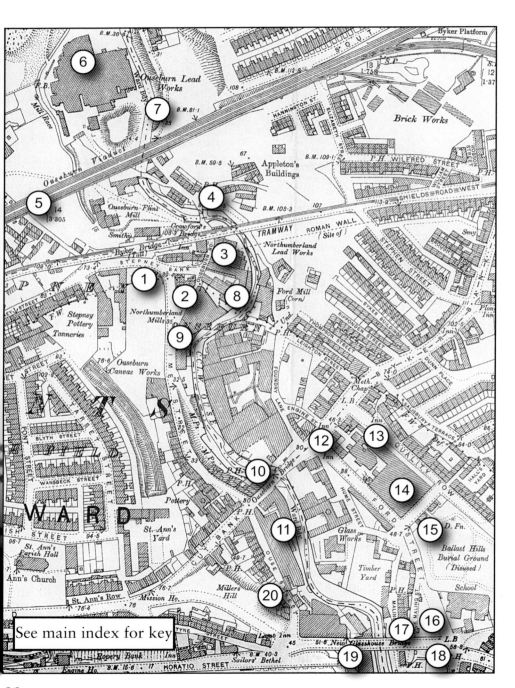

See main index for key

1. Stepney Bank

Before the opening of Byker Bridge over the Ouseburn Valley in 1878, Stepney Bank was a major route connecting Newcastle with Byker and beyond.

This busy thoroughfare, around three-hundred yards long, contained houses, tenement buildings, four pubs, a pottery, a tannery and a saw mill. Near the top of the bank stood a windmill that ground spent bark from the saw mill which was then used by the tannery in one of its processes. Other businesses in the street at this time included an abattoir, horse dealers and stables. Today Stepney Bank Stables on the site of the earlier stables is a registered charity that offers affordable riding lessons to inner city residents as well as enabling volunteers to gain practical experience of animal welfare.

Two of the four pubs survive as rebuilds. The Tanners Arms, first mentioned in the 1840s, remains at the top of the bank while the Ship Inn (about thirty years older) is at the foot. Apart from some of the pottery buildings little else remains of the original Stepney Bank.

One of the pubs that did not survive appears on this photograph, dated 1936, shortly before being demolished. Known as the Stepney Vaults and owned by Robert Deuchar Ltd, the pub is flanked by tenements where, in 1891, there were eighteen families (sixty-four people) living in either one or two rooms. The pub had originally been called the Brown Jug because of its position close to the pottery.

Modern and historic locations shown on the 18 Ordnance Survey Map (Locations are approximate)

2. Mill House, Stepney Bank

The compact triangular open area at the foot of Stepney Bank, now known as the Village Green, was once a place to live. Accommodation had either been in the double storey, four-roomed Mill House or in the tenement property to the rear as seen here in 1935, shortly before demolition. The lady at the door of Mill House was eighty-six year old Elizabeth Carr who, in her younger days, had been employed by the nearby flour mill as a 'bread sampler-baker' in her own kitchen. Part of Warburton's tenement building can be seen to the rear of Mill House. The tenement is said to have housed thirty-three people in eleven rooms for most of its 100 years.

To the right of the photograph is a glimpse of Byker Bridge (1878) and the Ship Inn, which can be traced back to at least 1811 and was rebuilt nearly a hundred years later. A section of the Co-op boot repairing factory, previously an abattoir and now apartments, is to the left. Not visible on this photograph but nevertheless remaining at the south end of the Village Green is the once tall chimney, now truncated, built in the early days of steam for the nearby flax mill.

Today, the Village Green with its fixed seating and tables is often used as an informal beer garden together with a small piazza at the lower end with granite seating in tiers facing the Cluny. Near the entrance to this area is a pair of stone plinths, each supporting a pile of stainless steel bowls similar in size and appearance to the earthenware bowls used in the toxic white lead industry (for the making of paints and varnishes) that once operated nearby.

The Stepney Vaults pub flanked by tenement buildings, 1936.

Eighty-six year old Elizabeth Carr stands outside the Mill House, 1935.

3. Ouseburn Farm, Stepney Bank

Top: *City Farm, early 1980s.* Below: *The visitor centre building is made mainly of environmentally friendly materials, 2016.*

As part of Byker's redevelopment in the early 1970s, it was decided to reclaim this former industrial site at the foot of Stepney Bank and create an urban farm providing educational and recreational activities for people, especially children, who normally would not have had any experience of rural life.

Clay and top soil were introduced to cover the polluted ground, then the steep-sided site was terraced. Livestock ranged from a couple of cows to hamsters and there was also space to grow animal food. In 1977, Newcastle's Lord Mayor opened the City Farm, as it was initially called, as a registered charity staffed by three full-time workers supported by volunteers.

Around twenty-five years later it was felt the farm needed an update. Buildings were demolished and the contaminated soil they stood on was replaced with a substantial depth of fresh earth. In 2006 a single building, constructed mainly of environmentally friendly materials that included a sedum roof and a rainwater recycling system, was opened. Now known as Ouseburn Farm, it comprises a visitor interpretation centre, facilities for education and training plus rooms for hire. A few smaller animals are kept on site and some ground is reserved for vegetables and other plants.

Also on this site is part of an earlier flax mill's engine house plus a few millstones thought to be relics from either a steam corn mill or a lead works that also once occupied this area. Attached to the remains of the former engine house is a stone plaque dated 1871 that previously belonged to the Northumberland Lead Works.

4. Crawford's Village and Bridge

This illustration is dated 1895 and features part of Crawford's village on the banks of the Ouseburn between Byker Road Bridge and the earlier Rail Viaduct (upper left). Crawford's Bridge is in the foreground. It is the oldest surviving crossing of the lower Ouseburn and dates from the early to mid-18th century. Grade II listed and constructed of coursed squared sandstone, it is named after Thomas Crawford, a former Byker pitman, who became landlord of the Loraine Arms, which is part of the long building immediately behind the bridge. At the centre of the bridge's west parapet, facing the road, is a mason's mark (a diagonal cross in a square) and directly opposite, on the east parapet, is an Ordnance Survey bench mark signifying its height above sea level.

The village streets, including Crawford's Row and Crawford's Lane, consisted of old, small dwellings with picturesque red tiled roofs but without basic facilities. All the structures except the bridges have been demolished and replaced with landscaping around the pillars of the 1982 Metro Bridge. The people in front of the bridge are probably housewives carrying out household washing but may alternatively be cleaning animal skins for local hide and skin merchants.

5. Ouseburn Rail Viaduct

The Ouseburn Viaduct, one of Britain's earliest railway bridges, opened in 1839 across the steep Ouseburn Valley and was part of a planned passenger line between Newcastle and North Shields. However there had been considerable opposition to the project, particularly from local proprietors of coaches and river craft who predicted 'thousands would be made workless'. Some even thought the Royal Navy would ultimately be weakened because it relied on those who worked on the river for many of their recruits. Boarding house keepers and shop owners at the coast were also worried at the prospect of losing custom and farmers along the route feared their cows would give less milk and hens would lay fewer eggs.

Although the line was short (just under seven miles) it was relatively expensive because of the need for several bridges, embankments, cuttings, a tunnel and two substantial viaducts, one at Willington Dene and the other at Ouseburn. Both of these viaducts were designed by the prominent Newcastle architects John and Benjamin Green (who also designed Newcastle's Theatre Royal), with similar features such as sandstone piers and abutments as well as the unusual use of laminated timber for their arches, a technique recently developed in France. The adoption of laminated timber (up to fourteen layers of three-inch planks pinned together with nails and bolts) was a cost cutting measure and the viaducts are thought to have been the first use of the technique in Britain. Thirty years later the timber arches of both viaducts were renewed in iron and at Ouseburn a plaque on the south side of the central arch records the manufacturer's name and date. A section of the original laminated timber is preserved at the National Railway Museum at York.

At a height of 108 feet above the Ouseburn and 918 feet long, the rail viaduct remained a toll bridge for around fifty years, imposing tolls for freight and rail passengers as well as for pedestrians who were charged 1/2d to use a narrow footpath (closed 1894) alongside the south side of the rail track.

The Ouseburn Viaduct was doubled in width to four tracks in 1887, re-decked in iron nine years later and in 1904 carried Britain's first suburban electric railway. A major refurbishment has recently been completed to enable this Grade II star listed structure continue as part of the main east coast rail link between England and Scotland.

Interestingly, during the initial years of the Newcastle and North Shields Railway its locomotives were made at the Forth Banks works of either R & W Hawthorn or R Stephenson & Co. They pulled carriages some of which were built at Atkinson & Philipson's works at Pilgrim Street (the former Odeon cinema site) on rails manufactured at Losh Wilson and Bell's Iron Works at Walker. Carriages were very basic at this time except for first class. Second class were 'open from the waist up' and third and fourth class 'had no doors and generally no roofs with seating arranged char-a-banc style in large trucks'. From 1868 it became compulsory to provide smoking areas on all trains containing more than one carriage of each class.

6. Ouseburn Lead Works

The painting by J.W. Carmichael, probably made in the 1840s, features a cluster of buildings in front of the Ouseburn rail viaduct known as the Ouseburn Lead Works. They were reputedly founded in 1774 by John James, a tobacconist, cheesemonger and bacon dealer in Newcastle's Side. The works continued here for well over a century before amalgamating with the Northumberland Lead Works and moving downstream to their site because of the infilling of this part of the Ouseburn Valley in the very early 1900s. On the right is the Stepney Windmill, which functioned partly as a corn mill until it was demolished to make way for Byker Bridge in the 1870s.

Ouseburn Road, to the left of the Ouseburn, was the major thoroughfare connecting the various mills and collieries upstream in Heaton and Jesmond with the river Tyne. The Busy Cottage forge and foundry, in what later became Jesmond Dene, used this road for access.

The buildings beyond the railway viaduct formed the nucleus of the flourishing Lower Ouseburn industrial and residential area.

Drawn by J.W. Carmichael and engraved by W. Collard, around 1840.

7. Ouseburn Culvert

For many years there was much debate as to how best to achieve easier access across the deep Ouseburn Valley between Newcastle and the expanding suburbs of Heaton and Byker. Byker Bridge had opened in1878 and was widened twenty years later but was not convenient for everyone. Should there be another bridge? Perhaps the valley could be infilled? Despite the view of many sceptics it was the landfill scheme that received approval on the basis that it would create more rateable land for the benefit of the city.

Work began in 1907 by the construction of a culvert to enclose the Ouseburn between Jesmond Vale and the rail viaduct into a shorter, and more direct route of around 650 yards. Built of reinforced concrete in an elliptical shape, the culvert measured thirty feet wide by twenty-one feet high by eight inches thick. During construction it became known locally as the 'worm'. Completion occured four years later at which point the Ouseburn was diverted through the culvert and the tipping of household waste began for which a charge was made.

The estimated time of five years to complete the landfill to a depth of around eighty feet dragged on to nearer fifty years and the planned developments, such as houses and business premises, never reached expectations.

During the Second World War, the culvert was adapted to become an air raid shelter for locals that also provided some sleeping accommodation and a shop. Later plans to host the British Empire and Commonwealth Games in 1966 never materialised and the idea of a Newcastle Municipal Athletic Stadium failed to progress beyond the provision of a cinder track. Today much of the area remains as open grassland with some shrubs and trees.

The photograph dating from around 1909 features the culvert or 'worm' under construction with the rail viaduct in the background. The remains of several homes and businesses, including the Ouseburn Lead Works, now lie beneath landfill.

8. Northumberland Lead Works, Stepney Bank

Already established in business as a wholesale chemist in Newcastle's Groat Market, fifty-year-old John Ismay decided in 1865 to widen his horizons by taking over the old flax mill buildings in the Ouseburn Valley (vacated by Clarke Plummer & Co.) to become a manufacturer of white lead for the paint industry. Both business interests were complementary since white lead was also used at that time in the preparation of some cosmetics and medicines.

The Ouseburn premises became known as the Northumberland Lead Works in 1871. Featured in the photograph, taken in 1973, is the stone plaque recording these details that is now attached to what is thought to have been part of the flax mill's engine house. This masonry can be seen within the grounds of Ouseburn Farm.

In 1884 the Northumberland Lead Works (John Ismay & Co) amalgamated with the Ouseburn Lead Works (James & Co) a few hundred yards higher up the valley which closed around 1905 and is now submerged beneath landfill.

The first serious rationalisation of the lead industry and the formation of Associated Lead Manufacturers Ltd in 1919 led to the closure of the Northumberland Lead

Works and the transfer of employees to the Hebburn site of Foster, Blackett & Wilson Ltd. The Ouseburn site was then occupied by Elders Walker & Co Ltd, the paint and varnish manufacturers, until the early 1960s, followed by the City Farm from 1977.

Also visible on this 1973 photograph is part of Byker Bridge and the Ship Inn behind a cleared area now covered by Ouseburn Farm.

9. Flax Mill and Flour Warehouse, Lime Street

A purpose-built flax mill opened in 1848 at 36 Lime Street to replace an earlier mill that had been severely damaged by fire. Designed by architect John Dobson for Clarke Plummer & Co, this new four storey mill (the fifth storey is a later addition) was built of ashlar stone with bold classical detail. The mill employed a few hundred workers (mainly female) in making linen from flax, which usually arrived on the Tyne as ships' ballast, and there was access to it from either Lime Street or the Ouseburn.

Adverse trading conditions in the late 1850s, as cotton replaced linen, led to the mill's closure and conversion in around 1866 into a flour mill for Procter & Sons who had moved from Willington Quay. Leethams of York took over the mill in 1896 and remained for the next twenty years as millers.

From 1931, J.E. McPherson, the wine and spirit merchants, used part of the premises as a bonded warehouse, which later became known as the Cluny because of a prominent sign on the building advertising the firm's special blend of whisky. Cluny is derived from the clan title of the McPherson family.

Around 1976, most of the premises were adapted for use as craft workshops to be run as a non-profit making workers' co-operative assisting young people to develop their talents. The building, protected by Grade II listing, also contains the popular Cluny pub.

The large photo on the next page, dated 1972, features the former flax mill (to the right of centre) with a flour warehouse to its left. Part of Byker Bridge is just visible at the upper right of the photograph.

In 1872 Procter & Sons, the millers, opened this purpose-built warehouse at 30 Lime Street next door to their existing flour mill with an internal passage connecting both buildings. Designed by the Newcastle architect Gibson Kyle, this new seven storey brick warehouse built around a framework of cast iron had access at the rear to the Ouseburn by means of a central gable hoist (still visible) for the loading of wherries as well as a front entrance on to Lime Street for horses and carts.

Henry Leetham & Sons, millers of York, took over the building in 1896 and remained for around twenty years. Various businesses used the premises during the next sixty years or so until in 1982 Vanessa Redgrave, the political activist and actor, bought the building to provide a retraining centre for redundant miners. Apart from a printing business (the Trade Union Printing Service), which operated for a few years, Redgrave's ideas were never fulfilled.

In 2005, after a few years of renovation and extensions, the building was opened as The Centre for the Children's Book by the Children's Laureate Jacqueline Wilson. Appropriately named Seven Stories, this popular, multi-award-winning venue provides a national home for British children's literature. It is a Grade II listed structure.

Next page, clockwise from top: 1) A view across the Ouseburn Valley towards Newcastle, the rear of warehouses on Lime Street dominate the valley. 2) Seven Stories on Lime Street. 3) The Flax Mill alongside the Ouseburn

10. View from Ouseburn Bridge

A view dated around 1900 from Ouseburn Bridge looking upstream, with a few wherries ferrying materials to and from the various industries that lined both banks of the Ouseburn. The river is tidal for a few hundred yards further upstream close to Crawford's Bridge.

In front of the distant buildings on the left is Lime Street, which derived its name from the 18th century lime kiln that once stood at the side of the Ouseburn near its junction with the slipway (still there), which connected businesses in the Lime Street area with river craft. The limekiln that burned limestone with coal was notorious for "the great nuisance it caused for the neighbourhood and those riding past" because of the smoke and toxic gases emitted.

Visible to the right is part of the former Ouseburn Engine Works which, with a workforce of up to eight-hundred employees, manufactured large products such as marine engines, locomotives and steam hammers for both the home and overseas markets. Today several small workshops occupy the site and a public footpath has been created alongside the Ouseburn with heritage information boards and metallic green bottles marking out a walking trail.

This view might have been completely different if an ambitious proposal from 1795 to construct a sea-to-sea canal from Newcastle to Maryport on the Cumbrian coast had gone ahead. Plans included the creation of a wet dock just north of Ouseburn Bridge with a series of locks rising to higher ground behind Gallowgate and Percy Street. Following delays due to rival schemes, bitter disputes and the Napoleonic Wars, the idea of a canal was abandoned in favour of a railway from Newcastle to Carlisle, which was completed in 1838.

11. Ouseburn Cattle Sanatorium

Before the development of general refrigeration, Newcastle was thought to be the second largest importer of foreign livestock in the kingdom. Most of the stock arrived from either Denmark or Sweden. There was already an animal sanatorium at Sandgate, but because of inadequate quarantine facilities Newcastle Corporation opened a replacement purpose-built sanatorium in 1876 on the west bank of the Ouseburn between Ouseburn Bridge and the river Tyne. These new single and double storey buildings were designed to hold a maximum of 635 cattle and 3,000 sheep.

Each week, large numbers of animals arrived at Ouseburn to be quarantined for twelve hours during which time they were examined by government inspectors for signs of disease. Healthy livestock were then released through local streets, either to market or the abattoir. This caused problems for local residents, who pointed out the danger of driving a large herd of cattle along narrow streets 'at a time when a great number of people on Sundays were going to or from church'.

Later, as vessels increased in size, the Ouseburn quay was proving to be too small and in 1885 a new, additional sanatorium opened at nearby St Lawrence – a site later occupied by Spiller's Flour Mill.

Following the introduction of refrigerated ships both sanatoria closed in 1893. From 1906 the Ouseburn site was occupied for over sixty years by a firm of confectioners (Maynards Ltd) and later for general warehousing. In 2005, most of the remaining sanatorium buildings were demolished. At present much of the site awaits redevelopment though some of the Maynard buildings have been restored as offices.

This 1899 photograph looks up stream to Ouseburn Bridge, with part of the sanatorium on the left and Liddle Henzell's glassworks on the right, both now demolished.

12. New Hawk Inn, Byker Bank

Located near the foot of Byker Bank, between Foundry Lane and Engine Street, the New Hawk Inn originated in around 1830, was rebuilt some fifty years later and remained one of a cluster of pubs within a very short radius of each other. The much older Old Hawk Inn, dating from the late 18th century, stood opposite on the other side of Byker Bank and both pubs co-existed for many years.

One of the better-known managers at the pub was Bob Gray a former sculling champion and a later referee of river races – he is the one wearing a white apron on this late 1920s photograph. Another celebrity manager was Seaman Tommy Watson, regarded as Byker's most famous boxer and the only Newcastle-born fighter at this time to have held a Lonsdale Belt as a British Champion.

Around 1932 Watson converted an upstairs room at the pub into a gym in preparation for his attempt at the World featherweight boxing title. The contest took place in New York in the following year but the former Royal Navy champion lost on points to the American 'Kid' Chocolate.

Part of the pub's business was to supply two pails of beer each day at around three o'clock in the morning to quench the thirst of night shift workers at the glassworks just across the road. On pay day another task for the manger was to collect 'tick' money from the night shift workers at the nearby lodging house, which often ended in a scuffle.

The pub closed in 1967 and this compact triangular site is now landscaped with grass and a few trees.

13. Quality Row

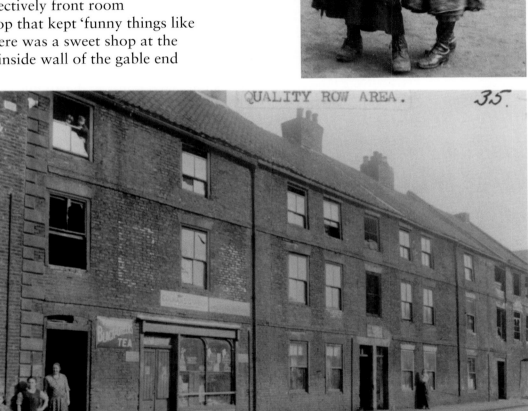

In response to a need to house a growing number of working families, several tenement dwellings 'of a superior type', were built in around 1800 in a new thoroughfare that led off Byker Bank. Appropriately named Quality Row, these homes were all on the north side of the street and overlooked unenclosed land until 1859 when Maling's new pottery (Ford A) blocked some views. Those living further along Quality Row, opposite the nonconformist burial ground, were more fortunate since that area remained open. In 1811, 349 people were living in thirty-three dwellings.

It is said 'the place was full of shops', effectively front room conversions, which included a chemist's shop that kept 'funny things like tapeworms and Siamese kittens in jars'. There was a sweet shop at the end of the terrace where a fireplace on the inside wall of the gable end enabled 'kids outside to warm themselves'.

The earliest Sunday School in the area was opened here in 1829 by W.B. Leighton, a local lay preacher, to teach children, many of whom worked long hours in nearby factories during the week, to read. The Steamboat Inn first recorded in 1841 and rebuilt forty years later was a popular attraction because of its quoits pitch. Finally there was the Mason's Arms, only a short distance from the Steamboat Inn, that originated as a beer house and was for many years the home of Jocker (John) Wood and family.

The photograph was taken in 1935 shortly before all properties were demolished. Today a scrap metal business covers most of the site and Quality Row is no longer a thoroughfare.

14. Maling's Ford 'A' Pottery, Ford Street

In 1815 Robert Maling transferred the family pottery business from Sunderland to a new factory at Ouseburn Bridge where it is thought there were improved trading conditions. Nearly forty years later, Robert's son, Christopher Thompson Maling, took control of the business and within a year or two had married Mary Ford, the daughter of an Edinburgh glass manufacturer. With the aid of her generous dowry he set about building a new, larger pottery nearby on a two-acre site at Ballast Hills adjoining the nonconformist burial ground.

Opened in 1859, the purpose-built pottery, equipped with the most up to date machinery powered by steam, could produce in one week what had taken a year at Ouseburn Bridge. It became known as the Ford Pottery (later Ford A Pottery) in a new thoroughfare named Ford Street. Maling concentrated on producing cheap commercial and industrial earthenware such as pots and

containers of all shapes and sizes. It has been estimated that Malings supplied at least ninety per cent of the pots for the UK's jam and marmalade trade and had an agreement with Keiller's of Dundee that lasted for around seventy years.

Poor trading conditions in the 1920s, largely caused by intense competition and the fact that glass was beginning to replace earthenware, were partly to blame for the pottery's closure in 1927. A scrap metal business now occupies the site.

The view below is looking along Ford Street towards Byker Bridge with the Ford A Pottery occupying most of the photograph. In front of the pottery, a corner of Ballast Hills Burying Ground can be seen with houses (demolished) for the Superintendent and Sexton just visible.

15. Ballast Hills Burying Ground, Ford Street

In 1549 an area east of the Ouseburn was acquired by Newcastle Corporation specifically for the dumping of ships' ballast. This district became known as Ballast Hills and was also 'used by local housewives for drying clothes and by courting couples who walked there after service on Sundays.'

It seems almost certain that a burial ground for non-conformists as well the poor of all denominations existed here from the 17th century. The earliest recorded headstone (now missing) is dated 1708 though it should be remembered that memorial stones were rare up to this period. A surviving stone to Thomas Davidson and his family dated 1742 is among many stones later used to form footpaths around the cemetery.

By 1785, complaints from surrounding residents about 'swine grubbing among the graves' led to them subscribing to have a low wall built to enclose the cemetery for the first time. A small dwelling for the grave digger was also constructed.

Around 1800, Ballast Hills was considered by one writer to be one of the largest nonconformist cemeteries 'almost anywhere', except Bunhill Fields in London, 'and where there are from twelve to eighteen, and sometimes double that number, buried weekly'. Another local observer wrote 'more bodies are interred here than in all the churchyards in the town'. There was no church or chapel at Ballast Hills and each interment incurred a fixed charge of six pence payable to Newcastle Corporation.

In 1826 the cemetery was enlarged to over three acres, a boundary wall (consisting of iron railings on top of a low stone wall) was rebuilt and two lodges replaced the earlier sexton's house. In order to cope with the volume of anticipated burials an additional privately funded nonconformist cemetery was opened at Westgate Hill in 1829.

Ballast Hills cemetery closed during the 1850s and around forty years later it became (and still is) a public park with headstones forming footpaths in the former burial ground. This open grassed area, is in Ford Street adjacent to the former Ouseburn School.

Right: *Tombstones form a footpath, image taken 1965.*

16. The Duke of York Inn, Back Maling Street

First recorded in the 1830s, the Duke of York Inn was sandwiched between Maling Street, near the Ouseburn and Back Maling Street higher up a hillside consisting largely of ships' ballast. A flight of a steep stone steps (still there) next to the pub connected both streets.

Jocker Wood, the all-round sportsman and champion quoits player, bought the Duke of York, his third local pub, in around 1900. All were managed by family members. His eldest daughter Lizzie Jane managed the Duke of York, his son Jocker Junior ran the Cumberland Arms for a number of years until his early death in 1912 while Jocker senior continued to live at the family home above the Masons Arms in Quality Row until his retirement at the age of seventy. In this family, any son christened John was automatically known as Jocker.

The Duke of York with its frontage on Back Maling Street was clearly named as belonging to Jocker Wood as can be seen in the photograph. Lizzie Jane and her dog, 'Jumper' are looking out of the upstairs window.

It was no great surprise that a quoit ground was opened on vacant land alongside the steep stone steps which was described as 'a big place all fenced in so that no one else could use it'.

Part of the building collapsed in 1946, luckily without any serious casualties, which led to the pub's closure, although the quoits pitch continued in use for a few more years. Today the site is derelict and awaits development.

17. Tenement Buildings, Maling Street and Back Maling Street

Tenement buildings were common in the Ouseburn Valley and particularly in Maling Street. In the 1841 census, when it was named York Street, there were 231 people living in fifty-eight tenements.

The central building in each of the photographs (five storeys in Maling Street and two storeys higher up in Back Maling Street) are two sides of the same structure that dates from at least the 1830s. Families lived in either one or two rooms with no yard and had the problem of having to carry water from a communal tap to whichever floor they occupied. At the 1881 census there were seventy-four individuals dwelling in fifteen tenements in this central building, which included an internal stairway accessible from the top or bottom (visible). Tenants at this time included a waterman, glassmaker, chainmaker, mangle woman and ship's carpenter as well as labourers and cartmen.

Both photographs, taken around 1935, contain parts of the Duke of York Inn shortly before it was demolished and in the Maling Street view some of the steps leading down to the Ouseburn remain visible. At present this hillside location awaits further development.

Maling Street.

Back Maling Street.

18. The Tyne, Maling Street

Situated near the mouth of the Ouseburn, the Ship as it was originally called, probably predated 1800 and is said to have been a favourite haunt of the Tyne's keelmen.

The present building is a rebuild following a major fire in 1895 and was described in an architectural book by Lynn Pearson as having 'an interesting combination of black and white half timbering on the first floor with a lightly classical ground floor combining red brick and fluted pilasters in fawn faience.'

19. Ouseburn Barrage, Maling Street

One of the most recent innovations in the Ouseburn Valley, near its estuary, is the new Barrage and Tidal Lock beneath Glasshouse Bridge. Opened in 2009 at a cost of £4.7 million, its prime purpose is to maintain a minimum water level of around eight feet in an area of the Ouseburn that is tidal. The aim is to improve its appearance and provide facilities for recreational activities such as boat trips, canoeing and small boat use at all times.

The photograph, taken shortly after the opening, highlights the 'guillotine' type rising gates at each end of the lock that enable small river craft to enter or leave the Ouseburn and at the same time allow a minimum level of water to be maintained.

20. Victoria Tunnel, Ouse Street

A few years after the Spital Tongues colliery opened in 1835, it was realised that it would be cheaper and quicker to transport coal to the Tyne by means of a waggonway beneath the streets of Newcastle directly to the mouth of the Ouseburn and so avoid expensive overland costs and congestion. Around two-hundred men were involved in tunnelling, in sections, along a two and a half mile route and then lining the interior with masonry and brick. The tunnel's dimensions were compact - just wide enough for a single rail track and sufficiently high for workers to operate. Excavated clay was used to infill nearby Pandon Dene.

In 1842, after nearly three years of construction, the tunnel was ceremonially opened by civic leaders to the accompaniment of cannon fire and live music. For around seventeen years, until the colliery became insolvent, the tunnel operated successfully with each 'coal run' consisting of thirty-two waggons each containing 2.5 tons of coal, enough to fill four keels waiting at the riverside staiths. Waggons descended from the colliery by gravity in about twenty to thirty minutes and after being emptied were hauled back by a rope attached to a stationary steam engine at the colliery.

Apart from a person attempting (unsuccessfully) to grow mushrooms in the 1920s, the tunnel then lay dormant for eighty years until the outbreak of the Second World War, when it was adapted for use as an air-raid shelter for an estimated 9,000 people. Today a seven-hundred yard section of the tunnel is open to the public at Ouse Street (booking is essential), where features such as blast walls, fittings for seats, bunks and chemical toilets can be seen. Ouse Street is the only remaining entrance to the tunnel out of the seven intially created in 1939.

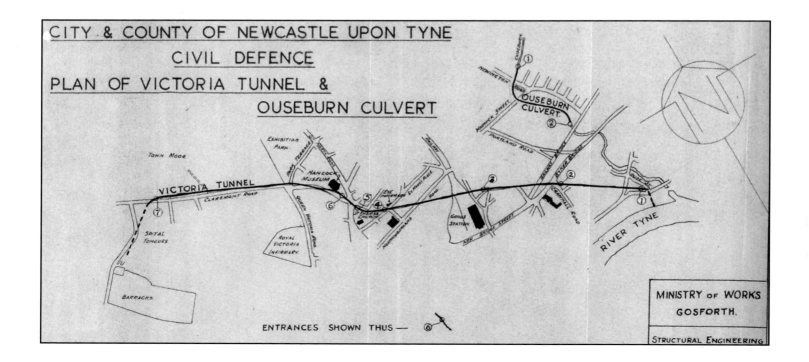

Selected Bibliography

Chapter One
Cinemas of Newcastle, Frank Manders
History of Wallsend, William Richardson
Bygone Byker, Sue Harrison and Dennis Yardley
Handbook to the Roman Wall, David J. Breeze
A celebration of the bridges between Tees and Tweed, Ian Hartley and Mike Brown
Coals from Newcastle, Les Turnbull
Hidden Gems of Tyneside, Derek Dodds
That'll be the Day, Tyne Bridge Publishing
From Roman Wall to Byker Wall, Byker Priority Area Team
Heavy Nights, Brian Bennison
Heaton Methodist Church Centenary Booklet, Norman Moore and Kirby Robinson
Domestos Ltd, Michael Byrne
Lost Railways of Northumberland, Robert Kinghorn

Chapter Two
Byker A-Z, Roger Fern
Byker Voices, Ken Groundwater
Pevsner Architectural Guide (2009), Grace McCombie
St Lawrence's RC Church, Charles Mundy
Windmills (Preliminary survey of Newcastle Mills) J.C. Day
Lost Stations of Northumberland and Durham, Alan Young
The Life of Dorothy Lawson, W. Palmer
Water to Tyneside, R.W. Rennison
Newcastle and Gateshead Architecture and Heritage, Faulkner/Peacock/Jones

Chapter Three
The Northumbrian Pub, Lynn Pearson
Constable, F.C. Moffatt
Ralph Hedley, Tyne and Wear Museums
Pictures of Tyneside, J.W. Carmichael/S. Middlebrook
Pottery Bank People, Newcastle City Libraries
St Anthony's Church of England Centenary Booklet
Pioneers of the North, P.Joannou and A Candlish
The Friday Book, P.Brown
Archaeologia Aeliana 2014, Richard Pears

Chapter Four
Lead Manufacturing in Britain, D.J. Rowe
Archaeologia Aeliana 1992, S.E. Thornthwaite
The Trademark of Excellence, S.Moore and C. Ross
The History of Maling, Tyne and Wear Museums
Railways of Northumberland and Newcastle, J.A. Wells
Tyneside, C.M. Fraser and K Emsley

One of several sculptures and artworks scattered throughout the Byker Wall area.

Index